For a century or more, political theology has been in decline. Recent years, however, have seen increasing interest not only in how church and state should be related, but in the relation between divine authority and political authority, and in what religion has to say about the limits of state authority and the grounds of political obedience. In this book, Nicholas Wolterstorff addresses this whole complex of issues. He takes account of traditional answers to these questions, but on every point stakes out new positions. Wolterstorff offers a fresh theological defense of liberal democracy, argues that the traditional doctrine of "two rules" should be rejected, and offers a fresh exegesis of Romans 13, the canonical biblical passage for the tradition of Christian political theology. This book provides useful discussion for scholars and students of political theology, law and religion, philosophy of religion, and social ethics.

NICHOLAS WOLTERSTORFF is Noah Porter Professor Emeritus of Philosophical Theology at Yale University, and Senior Fellow of the Institute for Advanced Studies in Culture, University of Virginia. He is author of several publications, including *Divine Discourse* (Cambridge, 1995), *John Locke and the Ethics of Belief* (Cambridge, 1996), *Practices of Belief* (ed. Terence Cuneo, Cambridge, 2010), and *Justice: Rights and Wrongs* (2010).

THE MIGHTY AND THE ALMIGHTY

An Essay in Political Theology

NICHOLAS WOLTERSTORFF

CAMBRIDGE
UNIVERSITY PRESS

CAMBRIDGE
UNIVERSITY PRESS

University Printing House, Cambridge CB2 8BS, United Kingdom

Published in the United States of America by Cambridge University Press, New York

Cambridge University Press is part of the University of Cambridge.

It furthers the University's mission by disseminating knowledge in the pursuit of
education, learning and research at the highest international levels of excellence.

www.cambridge.org
Information on this title: www.cambridge.org/9781107673809

© Nicholas Wolterstorff 2012

First published 2012
First paperback edition 2014

A catalogue record for this publication is available from the British Library

Library of Congress Cataloguing in Publication data
Wolterstorff, Nicholas.
The mighty and the almighty : an essay in political theology / Nicholas Wolterstorff.
p.   cm.
ISBN 978-1-107-02731-2 (Hardback)
1. Political theology.   2. Church and state.   3. Christianity and politics.   I. Title.
BT83.59.W65 2012
261.7–dc23
2012017168

ISBN 978-1-107-02731-2 Hardback
ISBN 978-1-107-67380-9 Paperback

Cambridge University Press has no responsibility for the persistence or accuracy of
URLs for external or third-party internet websites referred to in this publication,
and does not guarantee that any content on such websites is, or will remain, accurate
or appropriate.

Contents

Acknowledgments

I was invited to deliver the Stone Lectures at Princeton Theological Seminary in 1998, the centenary of the delivery of the lectures by the Dutch neo-Calvinist politician and theologian Abraham Kuyper (1837–1920). The project Kuyper set for himself in his lectures was to articulate the "essence" of Calvinism and point to the contribution of Calvinism to various aspects of the modern world.[1] The title of his third lecture was "Calvinism and Politics." In this lecture he offered an imaginative and provocative theological account of political authority. I decided to honor the centenary by reflecting anew on the relation between divine and political authority, incorporating into my discussion some reflections on what Kuyper had to say on the topic.

I was not happy with the lectures in the form in which I delivered them; so rather than preparing them for publication, I set them aside. Every now and then in subsequent years I returned to them, reorganized them, revised some passages, developed some points more fully, and so forth; but each time I once again found myself unhappy with the result. It was the stimulus provided by my participation in the McDonald Project on Christian Jurisprudence, led by Frank Alexander and John Witte of the Law School of Emory University, that made me take up the project yet one more time; otherwise I would have discarded it as a good idea that didn't work out. I thank Alexander and Witte, along with the participants in that Project, for their provocations; and I thank the faculty of Princeton Theological Seminary for the honor of their inviting me to deliver the Stone Lectures on the occasion of the hundredth anniversary of Kuyper's delivering them.

I am currently a Senior Fellow of the Institute for Advanced Studies in Culture at the University of Virginia. I warmly thank the Institute for the extremely pleasant environment it provides for thinking, reading, and writing, and for its financial support. My writing was also supported, when I was a Senior Fellow of the Center for the Study of Law and

---

[1] Abraham Kuyper, *Calvinism: The Stone Lectures for 1898–1899* (New York: Fleming H. Revell Co., n.d.).

Religion at Emory University, by a generous grant to the Center from the Alonzo L. McDonald Family Agape Foundation. I wish to thank Ambassador Alonzo L. McDonald, Peter McDonald, and the other McDonald Agape Foundation Trustees for their support and encouragement. The opinions in this publication are mine, however, and may well not reflect the views of the Foundation or the Center.

My title, *The Mighty and the Almighty*, is not original with me. It's the title of a lecture that Madeleine Albright gave at Yale University and that she subsequently used as the title of a book in which she expanded her lecture. I have no idea whether it was original with her.

Finally, I thank Terence Cuneo, Chris Eberle, Miroslav Volf, and Kevin Vallier for their very helpful comments on earlier drafts of the essay. The flaws that remain are to be laid at my door.

Introduction

In his book *The Stillborn God: Religion, Politics, and the Modern West*,[1] Mark Lilla observes that "In most civilizations known to us, in most times and places, when human beings have reflected on political questions they have appealed to God when answering them. Their thinking has taken the form of political theology. Political theology is a primordial form of human thought" (3–4). Lilla goes on to remark that "now the long tradition of Christian political theology is forgotten, and with it memory of the age-old human quest to bring the whole of human life under God's authority" (5). We in the West have been "separated from our own long theological tradition of political thought by a revolution in Western thinking that began roughly four centuries ago. We live, so to speak, on the other shore. When we observe civilizations on the opposite bank, we are puzzled, since we have only a distant memory of what it was like to think as they do" (4). Lilla's book tells the story of how "The Great Separation," as he calls it, came about.

These remarks of Lilla may lead some readers to infer that whereas once upon a time one turned to theologians and theologically inclined philosophers for a lively discussion of the authority of the state, now one looks to secular philosophers and

---

[1] Mark Lilla, *The Stillborn God: Religion, Politics, and the Modern West* (New York: Vintage Books, 2008). References are incorporated into the text.

I

political theorists for that lively discussion. One would look in
vain. The topic of political authority has very nearly fallen off the
agenda of theorists generally. In *The Authority of the State*, the
philosopher Leslie Green remarks about recent political theory
that "the general problem of political authority is rarely regarded
as being of primary importance." He says that "there would not
now be much agreement with T. D. Weldon's claim," made early
in the twentieth century, "that ['The aim of political philosophy is
to discover the grounds on which the State claims to exercise
authority over its members.'] Few of the most powerful contemporary thinkers . . . would accept this view."[2]

Lilla argues, correctly in my judgment, that at the core of
traditional political theology was the question of how God's
authority is related to the authority of the state. This present essay
is an address to that question. It is thus an essay in that for which
Lilla wrote the obituary, namely, political theology. More specifically, it is an essay in *Christian* political theology.[3]

Why would anyone want to resuscitate the moribund project of
political theology? Why not let this comatose dog rest in peace?
Why take up once again a project that for most people is "only a
distant memory"?

One reason for once again taking up the project of political
theology is that, for any theist who believes that both God and the
state have authority, the question of the relation between these two
forms of authority is inescapable. As Lilla remarks, "the question
of God can present itself to any reflective mind, at any time. And
once that question is posed, many others flow from it, including all

---

[2] Leslie Green, *The Authority of the State* (Oxford: Clarendon Press, 1988), p. 2.
[3] Though the term "political theology" is traditional for the discipline in question, it is
    somewhat misleading. Political theology is not theology with a political cast; it is
    theology of or about the political, more specifically, theology of or about the state.

the traditional questions of political theology. Political theology may not be a feature of every human society, but it is a permanent alternative to reflective minds" (19–20).

The answers given in the long tradition of Christian political theology to the question of the relation between divine and political authority cannot simply be rehearsed, however; the question has to be addressed anew. From around 500 CE until around 1600, almost all discussions in the Christian West of the relation between divine and political authority were conducted within the framework of the so-called "two rules" doctrine. As we shall see in due course, that doctrine is patently inapplicable to our present situation.

There's another reason for once again taking up the project of political theology. Political theology is not as near-dead as Lilla suggests. It's not vivacious, but it's also not moribund. The reason Lilla and most other scholars and intellectuals regard it as near-dead is that it's been flying under their radar. A book in political theology that has been enormously influential among Christian theologians, pastors and students ever since its publication in 1972 is John Howard Yoder's *The Politics of Jesus*.[4] Yoder holds that the state has power but no authority; hence there can be no such thing as an account of the relation between God's authority and the authority of the state. I regard that view as deeply mistaken. My aim is to develop an alternative.

In doing so I see myself as taking up a challenge that Jeffrey Stout issued to Christian thinkers in his fine book *Democracy and Tradition*. This is what Stout says in one place:

Every Christian is free to affirm God's ultimate authority over every political community, including his or her own, whether or not others

---

[4] John Howard Yoder, *The Politics of Jesus: Vicit agnus noster* (Grand Rapids, Eerdmans Publishing Co., 1972; 2nd edn., 1994).

agree. Indeed, Christians who make this affirmation are bound to infer that Christ is now ruling democratic political communities providentially, no matter who acknowledges or fails to acknowledge his authority. The central task of contemporary Christian political theology is to discern how Christ's rulership of such communities manifests itself.[5]

Stout would view what follows as well short of a complete political theology. And he would be right about that. I deal with only a few of the issues that he later cites as issues that, in his judgment, contemporary Christian political theology should address. The issues I do address seem to me fundamental, however; what one says about the relation between divine and political authority determines the shape of almost everything else. My discussion also falls short of being a complete political theology in that my treatment of the issues that I do take up cries out for further development at many points.[6] What I offer is not much more than a sketch of an account of the relation between God's authority and the authority of the state. But sketches have their uses.

To the disappointment of some readers, no doubt, I do little by way of engaging other theologians who have written on the topics that I will be discussing. In the opening chapters I discuss Augustine and John Howard Yoder because, in each case, their thought poses a challenge to my way of framing the issues. And I discuss Calvin's interpretation of Romans 13 and his version of the "two rules" doctrine so as to have before us an articulate and influential statement of the mainline tradition that I will be departing from. My engagement with Augustine, Calvin, and Yoder is thus in

---

[5] Jeffrey Stout, *Democracy and Tradition* (Princeton University Press, 2004), p. 103.
[6] From Chapter 8 onwards I appeal to natural rights; in my *Justice: Rights and Wrongs* (Princeton University Press, 2008) I develop a theory of rights. In Chapter 13 I employ a certain understanding of the liberal democratic state. I work out that understanding in my *Understanding Liberal Democracy*, ed. Terence Cuneo (Oxford University Press, forthcoming).

service to my systematic interests; in no case do I give a full presentation of their political theology as a whole.

Initially I planned to engage prominent contemporary thinkers whose views differ from mine. I wrote a draft of a chapter on Oliver O'Donovan's book *Desire of the Nations*; and I anticipated engaging at some length Karl Barth, Emil Brunner, and some contemporary Catholic theorists, especially Jacques Maritain and John Courtney Murray.[7] But eventually I came to the conclusion that though it would be illuminating to engage the views of these thinkers, pointing out affinities and highlighting where and why I disagree, doing so in this essay would clutter and impede the flow of the argument. Engaging those writers at length will have to await some other occasion.

As my thoughts developed concerning the relation between God's authority and the political authority of the state, I found a case for the liberal democratic state gradually emerging – albeit for a less individualistic understanding of the liberal democratic state than is common. This surprised me; I had assumed that an account of the relation between divine and political authority would be distinct from whatever case could be made for the liberal democratic state. Now I found the former topic segueing seamlessly into the latter. Thereby I unexpectedly found myself confronting the sour and caustic attitude toward the liberal democratic state expressed nowadays by a good many Christian scholars and intellectuals.

A standard line of critique goes as follows. Whereas in former days a political regime was the highest institutional expression of a community united in religion and morality – or in the days of

---

[7] The chapter on O'Donovan would have been a revision of my article "A Discussion of Oliver O'Donovan's *Desire of the Nations*," in *Scottish Journal of Theology*, 54:1 (2001), 87–109.

Christendom, one of the two highest institutional expressions, the church being the other – the liberal democratic state is the opposite of that. Though professing neutrality, it is in fact hostile to religion and destructive of morality, committed to secularism and to possessive individualism. It represents Weberian instrumental rationality gone berserk, a vast bureaucratic octopus, destroyer of tradition and community. It initiates and provokes war in order to stir up patriotism. The responsibility and loyalty of the Christian is not to this state but to the church.

Some readers will assume that I am speaking hyperbolically. Surely nobody actually says such things; or if they do, they don't mean them literally. Not so. All but one of these charges are documented and discussed in detail in Part 2 of Stout's book; no need to repeat them here. The charge that Stout does not take note of is the charge that liberal democracies initiate and provoke war so as to stir up loyalty. So let me quote what Stanley Hauerwas and William H. Willimon say on this point in their book *Resident Aliens*:

> States, particularly liberal democracies, are heavily dependent on wars for moral coherence. All societies may go to war, but war for us liberal democracies is special because it gives us a sense of worth necessary to sustain our state ... We are quite literally a people that morally live off our wars because they give us the necessary basis for self-sacrifice so that a people who have been taught to pursue only their own interest can at times be mobilized to die for one another.[8]

Someone who, like myself, concedes that there is truth in this biting criticism but who believes, nonetheless, that the liberal democratic state is a jewel of great price waits for a "however."

---

[8] Stanley Hauerwas and William H. Willimon, *Resident Aliens* (Nashville: Abingdon Press, 1989), p. 35.

We wait in vain. No "however" is forthcoming. Calvin was an extremely biting critic of the political authorities of his day; but always there was a "however." [Many if not most rulers are oppressive, says Calvin; however, government is an instrument of God's providential care for humankind.] Thus it is that Calvin says, in the concluding chapter of his *Institutes*, that "the Lord has not only testified that the office of magistrate is approved by and acceptable to him, but he also sets out its dignity with the most honorable titles and marvelously commends it to us" (IV.xx.4).[9] [Some people, says Calvin, hold that it is on account of "human perversity that the authority over all things on earth is in the hands of kings and other rulers." Not so. It is on account of "divine providence and holy ordinance" (ibid.).] "Accordingly, no one ought to doubt that civil authority is a calling, not only holy and lawful before God, but also the most sacred and by far the most honorable of all callings in the whole life of mortal men" (ibid.).

This citation from Calvin, with its hyperbolic praise of the dignity of civil authority, leads me to mention another thing that took me by surprise in the line of thought that emerged from my reflections. Since I regard Calvin as a typical representative of the traditional "two rules" doctrine, and since I know his texts better than those of anyone else in the long tradition of "two rules" thinking, I decided to take his formulations as representative of the tradition. (I also look briefly at Luther.) A historically oriented approach would survey a host of other figures as well; it would also look at the institutional documents in which "two rules" thinking was employed to deal with political issues facing the church.

---

[9] The translation of the *Institutes of the Christian Religion* that I will use is that by Ford Lewis Battles (Philadelphia: Westminster Press, 1950). References are incorporated into the text.

I knew in advance that what Calvin said could not simply be repeated in our day; it would have to be adapted to our situation. But given that I stand in the tradition of which Calvin was the most influential founder, viz., the Reformed tradition of Christianity, I anticipated that my line of thought would be "Calvinistic" in some way that I was not able to specify in advance. But the more I thought about the "two rules" doctrine and reflected on Calvin's articulation of that doctrine, the more convinced I became that the doctrine is not just inapplicable to our present situation but was deeply mistaken in its own day. Ironic that the most influential founder of the tradition in which I locate myself should be the one who draws the most fire in these pages.

It is not some generically theistic account of political authority that I develop in this essay — what would that be? — but, as I mentioned earlier, a *Christian* account. I invite others to listen in; but it is to my fellow Christians that what I say is most directly relevant.

Is there any reason for others to listen in? I think there is. In a participatory democracy such as ours, it's important that we each be open with and open to our fellow citizens concerning the deep sources of how we think about political issues. If there are distinctly Jewish ways of thinking about those issues, or distinctly Muslim or secular utilitarian ways, I want to hear about those. Not only does respect for my fellow citizens require that I invite them to tell me how they think about these issues and that I listen attentively to what they say; by their speaking and by my listening I get a sense of what they care most deeply about, and thereby some sense of what a politics that is fair to all would be like. And there is always the possibility of learning from them. I may not be able simply to take over what was said by someone of a different persuasion from my own; I may instead have to appropriate what

I discern her, in her own way, to be getting at, place it in a different context, formulate it with a different conceptuality. But that's how learning from others often goes, maybe usually.

Some will reject this invitation to listen in because they firmly believe that if political theology is not yet dead, it should be dead. I am thinking of those who reason along the following lines. Reflection on political issues in theological terms was rampant in the sixteenth and seventeenth centuries. The result was intense disagreement on almost every topic discussed.

Eventually the idea emerged, with John Locke as its preeminent representative, that the only way forward was to find some way of discussing political topics that did not appeal to our diverse religious and theological convictions but appealed instead to what we all share in common. In Locke's view that was reason, reason including our capacity for rationally apprehending the fundamental moral principles that he called "the law of nature." Locke's vision lives on, of a politics based on shared principles, its most prominent contemporary manifestation being so-called *public reason liberalism* of which John Rawls is the most prominent representative. Be done with political theology and thus with all the intellectual disagreement and social conflict that it creates. Embrace public reason liberalism.

My response is twofold. First, why not think about politics using the resources of one's own religious tradition *and also* seek as much agreement as possible with those who do not share one's tradition? Why not do both? Second, contrary to the original hope, the resolve not to think about political issues in religious and theological terms has not produced agreement, either on principles or on practice. The dream has failed. Not only is there intense disagreement between public reason liberals and those who reject public reason liberalism in general; there is also intense disagreement among public reason liberals themselves. Yet the discussion is conducted entirely in secular terms; no one appeals to theology. Are these present-day disagreements less widespread and less intense than the disagreements among the political theologians of the sixteenth and seventeenth centuries? Hard to tell.

Ans among
believers who talk
theologically

CHAPTER I

Framing the issues: understanding Polycarp

Late in his life the great but troubled American poet John Berryman published a slender volume of poetry titled *Love & Fame*. The last section of the book is called "Eleven Addresses to the Lord." Here is the last of those eleven addresses:

> Germanicus leapt upon the wild lion in Smyrna,
> wishing to pass quickly from a lawless life.
> The crowd shook the stadium.
> The proconsul marveled.
>
> "Eighty & six years have I been his servant,
> and he has done me no harm.
> How can I blaspheme my King who saved me?"
> Polycarp, John's pupil, facing the fire.
>
> Make me too acceptable at the end of time
> in my degree, which then Thou wilt award.
> [Cancer, senility, mania,
> I pray I may be ready with my witness.[1]]

The episode to which Berryman refers is the martyrdom of Polycarp, Bishop of Smyrna, on February 22, 156 CE.

Our knowledge of the martyrdom of Polycarp comes from the account of his death sent by "the church of God which sojourns in Smyrna to the church of God which sojourns in Philomelium, and

---

[1] John Berryman, *Love & Fame* (New York: Farrar, Straus and Giroux, 1970), p. 96.

to all the sojournings of the Holy Catholic Church in every place."[2] I propose framing the issues to be discussed in this essay by looking closely at this account.

The letter opens with the story of the martyrdom of "the most noble Germanicus" who "fought gloriously with the wild beasts. When the proconsul wished to persuade him and bade him have pity on his youth, [Germanicus] violently dragged the beast towards himself, wishing to be released more quickly from their unrighteous and lawless life." The letter reports that "the crowd, wondering at the nobility of the God-loving and God-fearing people of the Christians, cried out: 'Away with the atheists; let Polycarp be searched for'" (III.1–2).

Told about the call for his arrest that had erupted in the stadium, Polycarp, we learn, "was not disturbed" and "wished to remain in the city." His fellow Christians urged him to leave; staying in the city seemed to them tantamount to seeking martyrdom, of which they disapproved. So Polycarp fled and hid out on various farms near by. The police soon found him, arrested him, and brought him back to the city and into the stadium, whereupon there was "a great uproar."

The proconsul, Stadius Quadratus, urged Polycarp to recant and save himself from execution. Revile Christ, he urged, swear by the genius (*tychê*) of Caesar, and declare, "Away with the atheists" – that is, away with the Christians who deny the gods of the people. But instead of recanting, Polycarp gestured toward the crowd of "lawless heathen" in the stadium and, looking up to heaven, groaned and said, "Away with the atheists," referring to the people in the crowd. Then, rather than swearing by the genius of Caesar

---

[2] I am using the translation to be found in Kirsopp Lake, ed. and trans., *The Apostolic Fathers*, vol. II, Loeb Classical Library (Cambridge, MA: Harvard University Press, 1913). References are incorporated into the text.

and reviling Christ, he declared, "For eighty and six years have I been his servant, and he has done me no wrong; how can I blaspheme my King [*basileus*], who has saved me?"

There is a long and thick history of people who have resisted the demands of government and paid with their lives. That history of resistance and sacrifice continues into our own day. Some have resisted in the name of morality: government has ordered them to do or desist from doing what in good conscience they could not do or desist from doing. Morally heroic individuals up against the crushing power of government. Others have resisted out of loyalty to some group: their nation, their party, their band of revolutionaries.

Polycarp's resistance was different. He did not declare that obeying his own interior conscience had higher priority for him than obeying the proconsul. He did not declare that loyalty to his group had higher priority for him than whatever loyalty he might feel toward Caesar, the proconsul, and the people in the stadium. The voice of interior conscience, along with group loyalty of some form, may well have been present in Polycarp. But the explicit ground of his resistance was thoroughly heteronomous. He had a sovereign distinct from Caesar, namely, Christ. The proconsul was demanding that he renounce that sovereign. That he would not do, for his sovereign had saved him.

What would Polycarp have done had the proconsul only enjoined him to swear by the genius of Caesar and not also to renounce Christ? *Tyche* was the translation into the Greek of the day of the Latin *genius*, this translation being preferred over the traditional *daemon* because that term had acquired the connotation of something evil. A *tyche* was pretty much what we today would call a *spirit* – more specifically, a *patron spirit*. Cities were thought to have patron spirits; the view was gaining in popularity that the emperor had a patron spirit, a *genius*, a *tyche*.

The people in the stadium correctly understood the Christians to be deniers of all their familiar patron spirits and deities; that's what lay behind their charge that the Christians were atheists. At a certain point the people shouted at Polycarp, "This is the teacher of Asia, the father of the Christians, the destroyer of our gods, who teaches many neither to offer sacrifice nor to worship" (XII.2).

We can safely infer what Polycarp would have done had the proconsul only pressed him to swear by Caesar's patron spirit and not also to renounce Christ. Polycarp would have refused.

The proconsul, not willing to take Polycarp's initial "No" for an answer, persisted. Eventually Polycarp became exasperated. Look, he said, "you pretend that you are ignorant [of who] I am . . . I am a Christian. And if you wish to learn the doctrine of Christianity, fix a day and listen." Then you will understand why I cannot renounce Christ or swear by the *tychê* of Caesar.

Don't persuade me, "persuade the people," retorted the proconsul.

"I do not count them worthy that a defence should be made to them," replied Polycarp. You and I, though, could have a worthwhile discussion, "for we [Christians] have been taught to render honour, as is meet, if it hurts us not, to princes and authorities appointed by God." Polycarp's words indicate that he regarded the proconsul, and Caesar above him, as among the princes and authorities appointed by God to whom appropriate honor is due.

Things are getting complicated now. In declaring that he had a sovereign, Christ, distinct from Caesar and his proconsul, Polycarp was not implying that Caesar and his proconsul were not his sovereigns; he was not implying that Christ was his sovereign *instead of* Caesar and his proconsul. He was not suggesting that he was an alien in Smyrna, and that his political home was either somewhere else in the empire or outside the empire. No; he was a citizen of Smyrna; and the proconsul had political jurisdiction over

Smyrna. Polycarp was under *dual* authority. In his person, the authority of Christ and the authority of the emperor intersected. Given the command of Caesar's proconsul to renounce Christ, those two authorities had now collided.

Another complication, and irony as well. Princes and authorities are appointed by God, says Polycarp. In the authority of Caesar and his proconsul Polycarp discerned a duality that was invisible to the proconsul and the people in the stadium. The situation in which Polycarp found himself was that the civil authority appointed by God was ordering him to renounce Christ his king. Polycarp was not a polytheist. He believed that Christ was in some way one with God – though neither he nor anyone else had yet articulated how that was. Polycarp's situation was that the God who had appointed the civil authority was the king that the civil authority was now ordering him to renounce. Stadius Quadratus was ordering Polycarp to renounce the king who had appointed him, Stadius Quadratus, as a civil authority.

There's another duality in Polycarp's situation that we must take note of, a duality that does not get expressed in what has been transmitted to us of Polycarp's speech. The confrontation between the proconsul and Polycarp was not a collision between someone having authority and someone not having authority. Polycarp was a bishop of the church, exercising the authority of Christ over the church. An institutional conflict was taking place, invisible to most of the pagans in the stadium but not to the members of the church and certainly not to Polycarp. Two distinct authority structures were in collision, church and empire.

Again, a complication. Not only were the authority structures of church and empire in collision there in the stadium. Polycarp, unlike Stadius Quadratus, was located at the intersection of the two: bishop of the church and citizen of the empire. One person within two authority structures. Polycarp's entrance into the church by baptism did not undo his citizenship in the empire; it did not turn him into a resident alien. Neither did his ordination as bishop turn him into a resident alien. There have been regimes so hostile to the church that its members were deprived of political citizenship and either exiled or given the status of resident aliens. That was not Polycarp's situation. He, along with the other people in the stadium, was a citizen of Smyrna. One person, dual membership.

Another complication, along with irony: as a bishop of the church, Polycarp exercised the authority of Christ over the church; as an imperial authority, Stadius Quadratus was appointed by God. But Christ is God. There, in the stadium in Smyrna, two manifestations of divine rule, civil and ecclesiastical, in collision with each other.

The fundamental challenge facing the Christian thinker who puts his hand to articulating a political theology can now be simply stated: it is to understand the dualities in Polycarp's situation. Polycarp's situation is paradigmatic. One of the dualities in Polycarp's situation is a duality in the situation of every human being whatsoever: political authority mediates divine authority while at the same time being limited and placed under judgment by divine authority. The other duality is a duality peculiar to the Christian: as a citizen of some state he is under its authority, it in turn being under God's authority; as a member of the church he is under its authority, it in turn being under Christ's authority. And Christ is divine. Christian political theology aims at understanding these two dualities.

By no means would all who have thought about these matters accept this way of framing the issues. In the next two chapters I will address the major objections in some detail; here let me briefly mention two others.

Some will find it strange to think of the church in terms of authority. They think of the church as a voluntary organization devoted to sponsoring religious activities. A group of us find ourselves interested in religion, in particular the Christian religion; so we get together and set up an organization for holding worship services and for engaging in a bit of social action. We put in place some organizational structure, call a minister, place ads in the local press, welcome neighbors. We are off and running.

Everything about religion in America conspires to make one think of the church along these lines. Christ as king and the church as an authority structure are nowhere in view. The local government may decide to clamp down on our group for one reason or another – it doesn't like the architectural plans, doesn't like the fact that wine is served to minors, doesn't like the traffic jams. We may resist. But if we do, our resistance will be in the name of religious freedom. We will not declare that Christ is our king and that loyalty to our king requires that we not concede to the government's demands. No Polycarps among us.

Others will find it not strange but offensive to use the language of rule, authority, sovereignty, lordship, kingship, monarchy, in connection with Christ and the church. Such language is all too familiar to them, not strange at all. It must be rejected. Have we not seen more than enough of the evil effects of ecclesiastical authority? Christ came not to be served but to serve; his body, the church, is to do likewise. It was a mistake for Polycarp to speak of Christ as king. Savior, yes; king, no. Polycarp's mistake must not be perpetuated.

The abuses to which the objectors point are painfully real. Yet fidelity to Christian scripture requires that Christians join Polycarp in declaring that Christ is our sovereign. Our protests against abuses of ecclesiastical authority must not take the form of insisting that Christ has no authority but must instead take the form of insisting that those who perpetrate the abuses do not have Christ's authority to do so.

CHAPTER 2

Yoder's objection to our framing of the issues

In the Introduction I mentioned John Howard Yoder's immensely influential book *The Politics of Jesus: Vicit agnus noster.*[1] Yoder would object to how I framed the issues in the preceding chapter.

I said that in Polycarp's situation we can discern two dualities: the duality of the authority of the state mediating the authority of God, and the duality of Christians being under the authority of both church and state. I stated that a central part of the task of Christian political theology is to understand these two dualities. Yoder would reply that the dualities I claim to see are non-existent. The state has no authority. States have coercive power over their subjects; they do not have authority over them. Hence there is neither the duality of state authority mediating divine authority nor the duality of Christians being under the authority of both church and state.

Given the popularity of Yoder's line of thought, we must address his objection before we proceed to give our account of the two dualities.[2] The aim of my discussion in this chapter will be to show that Yoder's argument for there being no such thing as state authority is not successful. I will not take the next step of

---

[1] John Howard Yoder, *The Politics of Jesus: Vicit agnus noster* (Grand Rapids: Wm. B. Eerdmans Publishing Co., 1972). References are incorporated into the text.

[2] My discussion in this chapter is concerned exclusively with *The Politics of Jesus*, this being far and away Yoder's most influential work. A full discussion of what Yoder had to say about the state would have to take account of later writings as well.

arguing that the state does in fact have authority; that will be left for later, after we have discussed the nature of political authority.

Though Yoder regards the state as belonging to the order of creation and regards its continued existence as a manifestation of God's providential care for humankind, he never tires of excoriating creation-order theologies. The "theology of the orders of creation," he says, "has generally affirmed that Jesus Christ has little directly to do with them, but that rather these several orders (the state, family, economy, etc.) have an autonomous value unrelated to redemption and the church, by virtue of their being the product of a divine act of creation" (144).

Yoder's rejection of creation-order theologies takes the specific form of attacking the idea, prevalent at the time he wrote, that the ethic that Jesus taught and practiced and that Paul preached has little relevance to the problems that social ethics deals with. Social ethics, so it was commonly said, has to find some source of guidance in addition to Jesus and Paul – natural law, for example. Yoder's goal in his book was to show that this shortfall is entirely of the theologian's making. Jesus and Paul, rightly understood, give us a social ethic.

Yoder noted that what contributed to the supposed shortfall was puzzled dismissal of the language of "powers" in Paul's letters as outmoded and dispensable. "Since the onset of New Testament studies it has practically been taken for granted that when the apostle speaks about angels or demons or powers this is a dispensable remainder of an antique worldview, needing not even to be interpreted or translated but simply to be dropped without discussion" (139). But just when Yoder was becoming disturbed by the claim of shortfall, some scholars were developing a fresh interpretation of what Paul (and other New Testament writers) meant by "powers." And lo and behold, when these are placed side by side – the supposed shortfall for social ethics of what Jesus and Paul say, and the fresh interpretation of the language of powers – we see "that the unmanageable imagery [of the powers] has the same shape as the missing piece in the ethical puzzle" (139). So let us see how Yoder interprets Paul's language of "powers" and what he takes Jesus and Paul to be teaching concerning these powers.

Best to have before us a few of the New Testament passages under consideration. In Colossians 1:15–16 Paul says that Christ

is the image of the invisible God, the first-born of all creation; for in him all things were created, in heaven and on earth, visible and invisible, whether thrones or dominions or principalities or authorities – all things were created through him and for him.

In Colossians 2:15 we read that God

disarmed the principalities and powers and made a public example of them, triumphing over them in Christ [or, in the cross].

And in Romans 8:38 Paul says that

I am sure that neither death, nor life, nor angels, nor principalities, nor things present, nor things to come, nor powers, nor height, nor depth, nor anything else in all creation will be able to separate us from the love of God in Christ Jesus our Lord.

What are we to make of this language? Yoder acknowledges his indebtedness to the interpretation worked out by the twentieth-century Dutch theologian Hendrikus Berkhof in his booklet *Christ and the Powers*.[3] Berkhof held that Paul was probably using his variegated terminology – "angels," "principalities," "powers," "authorities," "dominions" – to refer to different sorts of entities; it's unlikely that he was using these different terms for the same

---

[3] Hendrikus Berkhof, *Christ and the Powers*, trans. J. H. Yoder (Scottdale, PA: Herald Press, 1962).

things. But be that as it may, says Yoder, "the best we can do today is to come to some understanding about[the general trend of meaning which the total body of thought has for us.]We may quite agree with Berkhof that Paul probably had . . . a very precise understanding in mind; but it could be well pointed out that it would hardly matter if he [Paul] had not" (137 n. 2).

What is "the general trend of meaning which [this] total body of thought has for us"? Following Berkhof, Yoder suggests that Paul is speaking about the intellectual, ethical, religious, political, and social structures that give order and stability to human existence. Or if someone objects that it is anachronistic to claim that Paul was employing the concept of structures, let the point be that "with careful analysis we observe that it can be said of all of these 'structures' what the apostle was saying concerning the powers" (143).[There is more to human reality than individuals and their actions. There are *structures;*]and "these structures are not and never have been a mere sum total of the individuals composing them. The whole is more than the sum of its parts. And this 'more' is an invisible Power, even though we may not be used to speaking of it in personal or angelic terms" (143).

What, then, was Paul saying about structures, including political structures, with his language of powers? Basically three things, says Yoder. First, that these structures, in their "general essence," are "parts of a good creation" (143).[4] They "were created by God.

---

[4] This point in Yoder, about the structures being "parts of a good creation," has been so often overlooked or neglected that it's worth quoting another passage to the same effect: "It is important . . . to begin with the reminder that [the Powers] were part of the good creation of God. Society and history, even nature, would be impossible without regularity, system, order – and God has provided for this need. The universe is not sustained arbitrarily, immediately, and erratically by an unbroken succession of new divine interventions. It was made in an ordered form and 'it was good.' The creative power worked in a mediated form, by means of the Powers that regularized all visible reality" (141).

It is the divine purpose that within human existence there should be a network of norms and regularities to stretch out the canvas upon which the tableau of life can be painted" (147). God did not *first* create human beings and then *later* create these structures. The structures are necessary conditions of human existence. "There could not be society or history, there could not be humanity without the existence above us of religious, intellectual, moral and social structures. *We cannot live without them*" (143).

Second, though these structures were created good, they

have rebelled and are fallen. [They did not accept the modesty that would have permitted them to remain conformed to the creative purpose, but rather they claimed for themselves an absolute value.] They thereby enslaved humanity and our history. We are bound to them; "slavery" is in fact one of the fundamental terms used in the New Testament to describe the lost condition of men and women outside of Christ. To what are we subject? Precisely to those values and structures which are necessary to life and society but which have claimed the status of idols and have succeeded in making us serve them as if they were of absolute value. (142)

Our "lostness consists in our subjection to the rebellious powers of a fallen world" (144).

Before we move on to what Yoder sees as the third aspect of Paul's teaching concerning structures, let us hold up to the bright light of day his way of describing this second feature, their fallenness. Our states, says Yoder, "absolutize" themselves, demand from us "unconditioned loyalty," "enslave us"; we are "unconditionally subjected" to them (143). Once the spell cast by the hypnotic language weakens, one is led to wonder whether perhaps Yoder is talking about some other world than the one you and I live in. Denmark, Canada, the Netherlands: do they enslave their citizens? Do they absolutize themselves? Are their citizens unconditional subjects? Why this aggressive language?

Yoder says that he does not want to get into the debate over whether the powers, as Paul understood them, are "personal demonic intelligences" (160 n. 28). He rather thinks "the student of the ancient world" will wind up less clear than "the person in the pew" as to "what would have to be meant by 'intelligences' or by 'personal.'" But Yoder judges that the issue is not decisively clear one way or the other.

Let's suppose that Yoder is right about this, that it's debatable whether or not Paul thought of the powers as personal intelligences – in our sense of "personal intelligences." [What we must not lose from view is the fact that Paul's way of speaking about the powers strongly suggests that they do have some sort of supra-natural status.]

But the structures that shape our existence are not supra-natural; the state is not supra-natural. In Paul's way of speaking there is thus an ontological *distance* between the powers and our social structures. We are justified in extrapolating from what Paul says to the conclusion that our states and other social structures are *under the influence* of fallen powers. But they are not identical.

Yoder identifies them. He acknowledges no ontological distinction between the Pauline powers and our social structures; he treats them as identical. The state "is an invisible Power," he says. This identification explains his rousingly negative language about states: states "absolutize" themselves, "enslave" us, demand from us "unconditioned loyalty"; we are "unconditionally subjected" to them. This is language appropriate to the fallen powers.

Now for the third aspect of Yoder's interpretation of Paul's teaching about social structures. What we have seen thus far is that, on Yoder's interpretation, social structures are Pauline powers that were created good but are now fallen. How, then, are we to understand the fact that after the Cross and Resurrection

these structures that are fallen powers still exist? Before the Cross
and Resurrection God was biding time, getting ready for the
battle. How are we to understand the fact that after the Cross
and Resurrection the structures that are Pauline powers still exist
and are still fallen?

There are two reasons why the states of the world and the other
fallen powers continue to exist. One reason is that states are an
indispensable component of God's providential care for humankind
in this time between the Resurrection and the Eschaton. States are
necessary for human existence in history; they provide the *order*
without which there could not be human existence in history.

States are fallen powers. They are evil. They oppress and kill
people. But what's the alternative? Chaos is the alternative.
Human existence is impossible in conditions of chaos. Human
existence needs order. And states – all states – secure order.
Willy-nilly they secure order. There cannot be a state that does
not secure some degree of order. So given the necessity of order
for human existence, states are historical necessities. Evil though
they are, their continued existence is a manifestation of God's
providential care for humankind. For God to abolish these structures would be to bring human existence in history to an end.
"Our lostness and our survival are inseparable, both dependent
upon the Powers" (143).

Yoder nowhere says that it is the task of the state to secure the
intrinsic good of social justice; neither does he anywhere say that
the states of our world fulfill that task to one degree or another.
States are for securing order. And order, on Yoder's view, is a
purely instrumental good. Yoder mentions no intrinsic good that
states achieve, only the instrumental good of order. That is no
accident; it follows from the identification of states with Paul's
fallen powers.

States are murderous and oppressive, but not necessarily so; though necessary for human existence they are not necessarily murderous and oppressive. This follows from the fact that they were once part of God's good creation. Given, however, that they are powers and that they are fallen, they are always in fact murderous and oppressive. And you and I are helpless to do anything about that; we do not have it in our power to undo the fallenness of the powers.

The second reason for the continued existence of those fallen powers that are the states of the world is that God is able to use the *particular* actions of *particular* states for God's own *redemptive* purposes. Assyria was an instrument in God's hand for bringing judgment on Israel (Isaiah 10); Pilate was an instrument in God's hand for bringing about the crucifixion of Jesus. The actions of Assyria, motivated by whatever warlike considerations the Assyrian king had in mind, had calamitous effects on Israel; the actions of Pilate, motivated by his refusal to stand up to the shouts of the crowd, had calamitous effects for Jesus. This is evident to any human eye. But the biblical writers were able to see behind what is evident to any human eye and spy the larger causal order within which these events were taking place. What they discerned was that not only were the Assyrian king and Pilate achieving their own murderous goals; *by way of* their achieving their goals God was achieving God's redemptive goals. "The church must be sufficiently experienced to be able to discern when and where and how God is using the Powers" (155).

We have looked at the three main aspects of Yoder's line of thought concerning the place of the state and other structures in God's "economy," a line of thought that he presents as an interpretation of Paul's teaching concerning the fallen powers. Note that nothing has been said about authority, neither anything about

God's authority nor anything about the authority of the state. Yoder thinks about the state exclusively in terms of power, not in terms of authority; and he thinks about the relation of God to the state exclusively in terms of power. The concept of authority nowhere enters his discussion.[5]

This too is a consequence of thinking of the state as identical with one of Paul's fallen powers. My Greek–English lexicon tells me that a good translation of Paul's term *exousiai* is "authorities." But there is nothing in what Paul says about the *exousiai* which suggests that they have the authority to issue directives to us, and so there is nothing in what he says which suggests that God has authorized them to do so. The powers are just that: *powers.* They exert power over us; they do not have authority. It's because Yoder thinks of the state as a fallen Pauline power that the question of whether the state has authority never arises for him. It cannot arise.

The opening verses of Romans 13 have often been interpreted as declaring that the existence of this government here and of that government there is a sign of God's providential rule of humankind. Yoder will have none of it. The existence of a particular government is a purely secular matter; there is no providential hand behind it. Providence with respect to the state is limited to insuring that some state or other exists; God then uses whatever state happens to exist for God's redemptive purposes. It's worth quoting at some length what Yoder says on the matter:

---

[5] Yoder's way of thinking of the role of Assyria within the providence of God is thus no different from the role of two female bears in the providence of God as we find it gruesomely described in 2 Kings 2:23–24. The prophet Elisha went "to Bethel; and while he was going up on the way, some small boys came out of the city and jeered at him, saying, 'Go up, you baldhead! Go up, you baldhead!' And he turned around, and when he saw them, he cursed them in the name of the Lord. And two she-bears came out of the woods and tore forty-two of the boys."

God is not said to *create* or *institute* or *ordain* the powers that be, but only to *order* them, to put them in order, sovereignly to tell them where they belong, what is their place. It is not as if there was a time when there was no government and then God made government through a new creative intervention; there has been hierarchy and authority[6] and power since human society existed. Its exercise has involved domination, disrespect for human dignity, and real or potential violence ever since sin has existed. Nor is it that by ordering this realm God specifically, morally approved of what a government does. The sergeant does not produce the soldiers he drills; the librarian does not create or approve of the book she or he catalogs and shelves. Likewise God does not take the responsibility for the existence of the rebellious "powers that be" or for their shape or identity; they already are. What the text says is that God orders them, brings them into line, providentially and permissively lines them up with divine purposes.

This is true of all governments. It is a statement both *de facto* and *de jure*. It applies to the government of dictators and tyrants as well as to constitutional democracies. It would in fact apply just as well to the government of a bandit or a warlord, to the extent to which such would exercise real sovereign control.

That God orders and uses the powers does not reveal anything new about what government should be or how we should respond to government. A given government . . . is simply lined up, used by God in the ordering of the cosmos. (201–02)

We have been reviewing and reflecting on Yoder's line of thought concerning the state and its place in God's economy. Let us now move on to consider his views concerning the stance that Christians should take toward the state. This will have the effect of both confirming and deepening what we have learned thus far.

"If our lostness consists in our subjection to the rebellious powers of a fallen world," what then, Yoder asks, can possibly be the "meaning of the work of Christ?" Subordination to these

---

[6] This is one of the few places in which Yoder uses the word "authority." Quite clearly it is being used as a synonym of "governance."

powers is a necessary condition of human existence; if we were not subject to structure, "there would be no history nor society nor humanity" (144). So Christ's work cannot consist of, and obviously has not consisted of, destroying the powers, the structures. Of what then does it consist? We learn from Paul that Christ "disarmed the principalities and powers and made a public example of them, triumphing over them." What does that mean?

What it means, says Yoder, is that without destroying the powers. Christ broke their sovereignty. How did Christ do that? Not by "some kind of cosmic hocus-pocus" (158) but by the way in which he related to the powers when living among us. First, Jesus *subordinated* himself. Instead of organizing a rebellion he "permitted the Jews to profane a holy day (refuting thereby their own moral pretensions) and permitted the Romans to deny their vaunted respect for law as they proceeded illegally against him" (143). Second, he subordinated himself *freely*. That is to say, he subordinated himself voluntarily rather than because he thought he had no choice; and he subordinated himself while retaining the conviction that the structures to which he was subordinating himself were fallen. In subordinating himself in these ways, Jesus lived "a genuinely free and human existence" (144–45).

It was by his freely undertaken subordination that Jesus "broke" the "sovereignty" (144) of the powers.

Here we have for the first time to do with someone who is not the slave of any power, of any law or custom, community or institution, value or theory. Not even to save his own life will he let himself be made a slave of these Powers. This authentic humanity included his free acceptance of death at their hands. Thus it is his death that provides his victory. (145)

Note well what Yoder is saying here. Christ altered nothing in the powers or structures themselves; they remain as strong and fallen as ever. Christ broke the *sovereignty* of the powers or structures, broke that sovereignty by *freely subordinating* himself to them.

The believer is to imitate Jesus. She is to follow his example and subordinate herself to the structures. At the beginning of Romans 13 Paul enjoins "every person" to "be subject to the governing authorities." Just as Jesus rejected the revolutionary option of the Zealots, so the believer is to reject the temptation to join the revolution. "The subordination that is called for recognizes whatever power exists, accepts whatever structure of authority happens to prevail" (198).[7] The subordination is to be undertaken *freely*, however, just as Jesus subordinated himself freely rather than because he thought he had no choice. And third, the believer is to follow Jesus in making clear that her subordination does not imply "active moral support or religious approval of the state" (201).

Free subordination to the state does not imply willingly participating in whatever the state does, nor does it imply willingly doing whatever the state asks of one; it does not even imply willingly participating in activities of the state that are essential to its maintenance of order. States in our world cannot exist without exercising the police function; but exercising the police function inevitably involves doing violence and harm to others, and Christians must refuse to do that. The function of exercising vengeance, which Paul in Romans 12:19 says belongs to God, "is not the function to be exercised by Christians. However able an infinite God may be to work at the same time through the sufferings of his believing disciples who return good for evil and through the wrathful violence of the authorities who punish evil with evil, such behavior is for humans not complementary but in disjunction" (198).

---

[7] Human reason tells us that *some structure or other* is necessary for human existence; what Jesus teaches us is that we are to subordinate ourselves *to the structures that be*.

When it comes to warfare, the dissent of the Christian will be yet more radical. Not only will she refuse to participate; she will insist publicly that it is not part of God's providential plan that states engage in such a function (203–05). If her state goes to war, she will not only refuse to participate but will make clear her disapproval of such action. Yet even in time of war she will freely subordinate herself. She will neither try to overthrow her government nor try to escape its jurisdiction.

These principles constitute the parameters of the Christian's mode of subordination to the state. The believer will not participate in either policing or warfare; and of warfare she will publicly express her systematic disapproval. The question that remains is, what is the Christian's mode of subordination within those parameters? What exactly does subordination in freedom amount to? What are the guidelines?

Yoder takes note of some points at which the Christian's stance toward the state requires critical discrimination. If we are to obey our states on some matters but not others, we have to exercise critical discrimination (207–09). So too, if we are "to contribute to the creation of structures more worthy of human society," we have to exercise critical discrimination (156). Where do we get the principles for making such discriminations? Where do we look for guidance?

Yoder does not say; and that is astonishing. Recall that *The Politics of Jesus* was written as a polemic against those theologians who thought that when it comes to social ethics, we must find sources of guidance in addition to Jesus and Paul. The argument of the book is that Jesus and Paul, rightly understood, are enough; no need to supplement their teaching with an appeal to natural law or anything else. So what do we learn from Jesus and Paul? We learn that we are to *subordinate ourselves in freedom* to the structures within which we find ourselves, including the political structures. This includes making up one's own mind on the political issues of the day rather than running with the crowd. But on where one looks for guidance in making up one's own mind, Yoder tells us next to nothing. What we learn from Jesus proves to be almost exclusively about free subordination as such; we get no guidance for living out our own particular mode of free subordination.

I think it is impossible to finish Yoder's chapter on "Revolutionary Subordination" without concluding that the free subordination he has in mind comes to nothing more than free subordination, *period.* That's why we get no guidance for living out some particular mode of subordination. The structure of marriage remains the same; but now the wife subordinates herself *in freedom* to that structure. The structure of a slave economy remains the same; but now the slave subordinates himself *in freedom* to that structure. And so on.[8] A most ironic outcome for someone who opened the discussion by presenting himself as unremittingly hostile to every ethic of inwardness!

The closest Yoder comes to offering a principle for Christian social ethics that goes beyond the abstract principle of free subordination is when he says that "the Christian is called to view social status from the perspective of maximizing freedom. One who is given an opportunity to exercise more freedom should do so, because we are called to freedom in Christ" (182). The suggestion

---

[8] Consider this passage: "The subordinate person becomes a free ethical agent in the act of voluntarily acceding to subordination in the power of Christ instead of bowing to it either fatalistically or resentfully. The claim is not that there is immediately a new world regime which violently replaces the old; rather, the old and the new order exist concurrently on different levels" (186). And this passage: "The wife or child or slave who can accept subordination because 'it is fitting in the Lord' has not forsaken the radicality of the call of Jesus; it is precisely this attitude toward the structures of this world, this freedom from needing to smash them since they are about to crumble anyway, which Jesus has been the first to teach and in his suffering to concretize" (187). Why is *smashing* the only alternative?

is never developed. Does the freedom to which the Christian is called in Christ imply that she should struggle for liberal democracies as opposed, say, to monarchies? Yoder does not say, nor does anything he says imply an answer. And in any case, he undercuts the thought that maximizing freedom is the fundamental principle for a Christian social ethic by immediately going on to say that the "freedom [to which we are called in Christ] can already become real within one's present status by voluntarily accepting subordination, in view of the relative unimportance of such social distinctions when seen in the light of the coming fulfillment of God's purposes" (182). I submit that there is nothing more to Yoder's social ethic than subordination in freedom – no guidance for critical discrimination concerning what states do, no guidance for pressing states toward becoming more just.

Yoder and his many followers would protest that I am neglecting the heart of the matter. In addition to subordinating herself in freedom to the structures of the ambient society, the Christian participates in that new community which is the church. Participation in the life of the church is the primary way in which Christians loosen the grip of those powers that are social structures; and that participation is by no means all inward. The "very existence of the church," says Yoder, "is its primary task. It is in itself a proclamation of the lordship of Christ to the powers from whose dominion the church has begun to be liberated. The church does not attack the powers; this Christ has done. The church concentrates upon not being seduced by them. By existing the church demonstrates that their rebellion has been vanquished" (150).[9] Agency proves not to be out of the hands of the powerless after all.

---

[9] The "primary social structure through which the gospel works to change the structures is that of the Christian community" (154).

One might ask how Yoder can say this about the church, given the theses he has defended. The church has human beings as its members, so the church requires structure; that is the application to the church of Yoder's principle concerning the need for structure. But if structures in general are fallen powers, then ecclesiastical structures are fallen powers as well. So presumably the paradigm of subordination in freedom applies as much to the Christian's conduct within the church as it does to the Christian's conduct within the structures of the ambient society.

Though it is astonishing, given the program of the book, that Yoder's paradigm should prove to be one more example of a social ethic of inwardness, it is nonetheless easy to see why it turned out that way. To think of political structures as fallen powers, and then to confine one's political theology to looking at the state through the lens of Paul's teaching concerning the powers, is to leave oneself without any source of guidance for critical discrimination in one's exercise of subordination. Nowhere does Paul urge critical discrimination in dealing with the fallen powers; nowhere is Jesus described as exercising such discrimination. Of course not. Jesus *opposes* and *conquers* the powers.

The lack of guidance for life within the parameters proves starkly evident in a passage about what Yoder calls "social discernment." Social discernment, he says,

is not simply a way of helping the needy with their social problems . . . nor does it mean simply to guide individual Christians by helping them to do good deeds or to avoid sin. It is rather a part of Christians' proclamation that the church is under orders to make known to the Powers . . . the fulfillment of the mysterious purposes of God . . . by means of Jesus in whom their rebellion has been broken and the pretensions they had raised have been demolished. (156)

True; social discernment is not *simply* a way of helping the needy nor *simply* a way of guiding individuals. But is it not *also* a way of helping the needy and *also* a way of guiding individuals? Is it *simply* the proclamation that the sway of the powers has been broken in Christ?

In the Epilogue to the chapter on "Christ and Power," written some twenty years after the original publication of *The Politics of Jesus*, Yoder remarks that "The vision of a dialectical interlocking of created goodness and rebelliousness, in what makes the world the way it is, has been found illuminating by many" (159). To this he adds that the "Pauline perspective is ... clear about the intrinsic complexities of institutional and psycho-dynamic structures, such that basically good creaturely structures can nonetheless be oppressive" (161). If this thought had been developed, that the "basically good creaturely structure" that is the state can "nonetheless be oppressive," a very different line of thought would have emerged from that which Yoder develops in *The Politics of Jesus*. Developing this alternative line of thought would have required saying much more about the state than can be said by regarding it as one of Paul's fallen powers. Or rather: it would have required recognizing that states are not fallen powers. *Subject* to the wiles of fallen powers, but not *identical with* fallen powers.

CHAPTER 3

The "two cities" objection to our framing of the issues

Our opening chapter was devoted to framing the issues. Extrapolating from Polycarp's situation, I suggested that central to a Christian theological account of the state is an understanding of the duality of state authority mediating divine authority and an understanding of the duality of Christians being under the authority of both church and state.

In the preceding chapter we addressed John Howard Yoder's rejection of this way of framing the issues. The state has no authority, says Yoder; hence the dualities do not exist. In this chapter we will look at another objection to my way of framing the issues. In this case, too, it's the popularity of the objection in certain quarters that makes it important to address the objection rather than brushing it aside.

The objection I have in mind comes from those who embrace what I shall call, using Augustine's terminology, the "two cities" doctrine.[1] The "two cities" doctrine as such is noncommittal on one of the two dualities that I have identified, the duality of state authority mediating divine authority. But it disputes my identification of the other duality.

---

[1] The "two cities" doctrine is not to be identified with what was traditionally called the "two kingdoms" or "two rules" doctrine. I will be discussing that doctrine in Chapters 7 and 12.

The doctrine comes in two versions. One version holds that Christians are not under the authority of both church and state because civil governments lack authority to govern Christians. Civil governments do in fact govern Christians, obviously. But they have no authority to do so. Hence Christians are not under dual authority. They are under the authority of the church but not under the authority of the state.

The more common version concedes that the state has authority to govern Christians but contests my way of describing that authority. When analyzing Polycarp's situation, I said that Polycarp was under the authority of the emperor because he was a citizen of Smyrna and Smyrna was a city within the empire, and that he saw himself this way. So too for me: I am under the authority of the United States government because I am an American citizen. The objector holds that the authority that civil governments have over Christians should not be thought of as the authority of a state over its citizens but as the authority a state has over aliens residing or traveling in its territory. Whatever their legal status, Christians should think of themselves, and as far as possible comport themselves, as aliens, feeling no more loyalty to the regime and no more responsibility for it than would an alien. For in fact they have no more responsibility for the regime than an alien has. The following passage from Hauerwas and Willimon's *Resident Aliens* is a clear expression of this second version of the doctrine:

We believe that the designations of the church as a colony and Christians as resident aliens are not too strong for the modern American church – indeed, we believe it is the nature of the church, at any time and in any situation, to be a colony. Perhaps it sounds a bit overly dramatic to describe the actual churches you know as colonies in the middle of an alien culture. But we believe that things have changed for the church residing in

America and that faithfulness to Christ demands that *we* either change or else go the way of all compromised forms of the Christian faith.[2]

There have been, and there still are, states that regard the Christians in their midst as aliens – or if not precisely as aliens, as some sort of foreign body whose presence is to be at most tolerated. The second version of the "two cities" doctrine is the correct way of thinking about that sort of situation. But it is clear from the passage just quoted that Hauerwas and Willimon hold that in whatever political jurisdiction Christians find themselves, they should think of themselves as aliens and as far as possible comport themselves thus. Though I am a citizen of the American state and dwell within its territorial jurisdiction, I should nonetheless think of myself as a resident alien and comport myself as such. It is this universalized version of the doctrine that is my concern in this chapter.

Augustine was the first to articulate the "two cities" doctrine. Since his influence on those who think along these lines remains enormous, I think it best to go back and see how he developed and defended the doctrine. So far as I have been able to determine, nothing Augustine says commits him to either of the two versions of the doctrine – though I would guess that it was probably the second version that he had in mind.

"Two cities . . . have been created by two loves," says Augustine,

the earthly by love of self extending even to contempt of God, and the heavenly by love of God extending to contempt of self. The one, therefore, glories in itself, the other in the Lord; the one seeks glory from men, the other finds its highest glory in God, the Witness of the conscience. The one lifts up its head in its own glory, the other says to its God, "Thou art my glory, and the lifter up of mine head." In the Earthly City, princes are as much mastered by the lust for mastery as the nations

[2] Stanley Hauerwas and William H. Willimon, *Resident Aliens* (Nashville: Abingdon Press, 1989), p. 12.

which they subdue are by them; in the Heavenly, all serve one another in charity, rulers by their counsel and subjects by their obedience. (*De civitate dei*, xiv.28)[3]

Though there is no overlap in membership between the heavenly city and the earthly city, given that membership in these two peoples is determined by two opposing kinds of love, the members of the two cities are commingled in this present age.[4] This commingling takes the form of members of the two cities living in the same neighborhoods, buying food at the same stores, working together in the same enterprises, and so forth. But it also takes the more problematic form that Augustine describes in these words:

> We see now a citizen of Jerusalem, a citizen of the Kingdom of heaven, holding some office upon earth; as for example, wearing the purple, serving as magistrate, as aedile, as proconsul, as Emperor, directing the earthly republic; but he hath his heart above if he is a Christian, if he is of the faithful, if he despiseth those things wherein he is and trusteth in that wherein he is not yet ... Let us therefore not despair of the citizens of the Kingdom of heaven when we see them engaged in the affairs of Babylon, doing something terrestrial in a terrestrial republic; nor again let us forthwith congratulate all men whom we see engaged in celestial matters for even the sons of the pestilence sit sometimes in the seat of Moses. (*Enarrationes in Psalmos*, li.6; Przywara, 270)

"Babylon" was a term that Augustine sometimes used to refer to the earthly city. "Two loves make up these two cities: love of God maketh Jerusalem, love of the world maketh Babylon" (*Enarrationes in Psalmos*, lxiv.2; Przywara, 267). So what are we

---

[3] The translation I am using is *The City of God against the Pagans*, trans. and ed. R.W. Dyson (Cambridge University Press, 1998).

[4] "These two kinds of love distinguish the two cities established in the human race ... in the so to speak commingling of which the ages are passed" (*De genesi ad litteram libri duodecim*, xv.20). The translation of this passage, and of all the Augustine passages in this chapter not from *The City of God*, is from Erich Przywara, SJ, ed. and trans., *An Augustine Synthesis* (New York: Sheed & Ward, 1936).

to make of his saying that citizens of the kingdom of heaven
sometimes hold an office in the empire and are thereby involved
in "the affairs of Babylon"? If holding an office in the empire
makes one involved in the affairs of the earthly city, how can a
citizen of Jerusalem who has "his heart above" possibly hold such
an office?

Augustine was tacitly distinguishing between, on the one hand,
the earthly city as a people of a certain sort and, on the other hand,
the imperial administration, and tacitly assuming that the latter is the
government of the former. The imperial administration is the
government of the earthly city; as such it is "engaged in the affairs
of Babylon." Sometimes under duress, sometimes voluntarily,
Christians find themselves in the ambiguous situation of occupying
a position in this government. That does not make them members of
the earthly city itself, members of that people; that's impossible.
Rather, they occupy a position in the government of the earthly city.

When a Christian occupies a position in the imperial administration he will "despise" the affairs in which he is engaged, for
they are the affairs of Babylon, not the affairs of his own city,
Jerusalem. However, this attitude on his part will be tempered by
the realization that the imperial government does maintain a
degree of order without which life in general, including the life
of his own city, the heavenly city, would be impossible. For this
reason, the members of the heavenly city do "not hesitate to obey
the laws of the earthly city, whereby the things necessary for the
support of this mortal life are administered. In this way, then, since
this mortal condition is common to both cities, a harmony is
preserved between them with respect to the things which belong
to this condition" (*City of God*, XIX.17).

Not only does the commingling of the two cities sometimes take
the ambiguous form of members of the heavenly city occupying

positions in the government of the earthly city; it also sometimes takes the equally ambiguous form of [members of the earthly city holding "pastoral chairs" in the church.]

> There are some who hold pastoral chairs that they may shepherd the flock of Christ, others fill them that they may enjoy the temporal honours and secular advantages of their office. It must needs happen that these two kinds of pastors, some dying, others succeeding them, should continue in the Catholic church to the end of time and the judgment of the Lord. (*Epistolae*, CCVIII.2, 3; Przywara, 258)

As Augustine put it at the end of a passage quoted earlier, "even the sons of the pestilence sit sometimes in the seat of Moses."

To make sense of this we must go beyond what Augustine explicitly says to draw a distinction parallel to that made above between the earthly city and its government. We must distinguish between the people that is the heavenly city, on the one hand, and the office or chair of pastor, on the other; the pastoral offices of the church constitute the government of the heavenly city. Members of the earthly city are to be found occupying offices in the government of the heavenly city. That does not make them members of the heavenly city, for that's impossible; they occupy positions in the government of the heavenly city. As such, they are interlopers. For whereas it is the task of those who hold pastoral offices to tend to the affairs of the heavenly city, these people have no intrinsic interest in those affairs. They may well be hostile to them.

Here is how Augustine puts it all together:

> There is today, in this age, a terrestrial kingdom where dwells also the celestial kingdom. Each kingdom – the terrestrial kingdom and the celestial, the kingdom to be rooted up and that to be planted for eternity – has its various citizens. Only in this world the citizens of each kingdom are mingled; the body of the terrestrial kingdom and the body of the celestial

kingdom are commingled. The celestial kingdom groans amid the citizens of the terrestrial kingdom, and sometimes (for this too must not be hushed) the terrestrial kingdom doth in some manner exact service from the citizens of the kingdom of heaven and the kingdom of heaven does exact service from the citizens of the terrestrial kingdom. (*Enarrationes in Psalmos*, LI.4; Przywara, 271)

The picture is of two distinct peoples, their peoplehood defined by their religio-moral unity, each having its own government. Here in this present age the members of these two peoples are commingled. They live and work among each other; and every now and then members of one city occupy positions in the government of the other.

Augustine's delineation of the two cities has problems. Where, for example, do the faithful Jews fit in? Surely they do not belong to the earthly city. But the institutional church is not their government. They have no place in the scheme; their position is anomalous. We can pass by those problems, however. For our purposes here the question to ask is, why did Augustine hold that the imperial administration was the government of the earthly city, the pagans? Why did he not hold instead that it was the government of everybody, pagans, Christians, Jews, everybody? The members of the church constitute a distinct religious community, a distinct people,[5] and the offices of the church are the governance structure of this people. But why hold that the imperial administration is the government of only those people who are not members of the church? Since our "mortal condition is common to both cities" and since the imperial administration tends to that common condition, why not hold, as Polycarp quite clearly did, that the imperial administration has the authority and responsibility to govern the members of both cities and that its affairs are the affairs of everybody?

[5] In the second chapter of the New Testament book of 1 Peter, the writer calls Christians "a chosen race" (*genos*), "a holy nation" (*ethnos*), "God's own people" (*laos*).

I know of no passage in which Augustine addressed this issue. But I think we can surmise why he thought as he did and not along these alternative lines. Christians of the first several centuries found the imperial Roman government suffused with paganism; paganism was, as it were, the established religion. In such a situation it was eminently plausible to think of the imperial government as government of and for the pagans. That appears not to have been how Polycarp was thinking; but it was surely a plausible way of thinking. Consider, as an analogue, a present-day Muslim state; such a state is plausibly thought of as government of and for Muslims. There may be non-Muslims within its territorial jurisdiction; but they are a foreign body – aliens, or whatever.

What would Augustine have said had he lived to see the Christianizing of Europe, or had he lived to see the emergence of a modern democratic state that guarantees to all citizens free exercise of their religion and that forbids the establishment of any religion? There's no way of telling.

Augustine framed the "two cities" doctrine in the context of the empire that he knew and did not undertake to apply it beyond that; it was left for later writers to universalize the doctrine. Some writers have defended universalizing the doctrine by arguing that every state does in fact implicitly establish some non-Christian religion or life-orientation; every state is in fact the state of and for some non-Christian religio-ethical community. Beneath the surface they are all anti-Christian. Other writers have defended universalizing the doctrine by pointing to various passages in the New Testament which teach, so they say, that Christians should regard and comport themselves as resident aliens.[6] An adequate

---

[6] Sometimes it is said that an implication of being baptized is that one should regard and comport oneself as a resident alien in whatever political jurisdiction one finds oneself. Hauerwas and Willimon, in *Resident Aliens*, say that "In baptism our citizenship is

address to the former line of defense would require an essay of its own; the latter can be addressed more briefly.

Prominent among the passages commonly cited is the passage in the First Letter of Peter where the author says, "Beloved, I beseech you as resident aliens [*paroikoi*] and exiles [*parepidemoi*] ... to maintain good conduct among the Gentiles" (2:11). In thus addressing his readers, the author is recalling the opening of his letter, where he describes his addressees as "elect exiles [*parepidemoi*] of the dispersion in Pontus, Galatia, Cappadocia, Asia, and Bithynia."

I think it exceedingly unlikely that the author was suggesting that Christians in general should regard and comport themselves as if they were exiles or resident aliens wherever they find themselves. His letter was addressed to Jewish Christians who were members of the diaspora, Jews "elect" in Christ who were political exiles from their homeland and living as exiles or resident aliens among Gentiles in Pontus, Galatia, Cappadocia, Asia, and Bithynia. Relatively few of us who now read his words find ourselves in such a situation. Violence over the past century has produced, and continues to produce, large numbers of exiles, Christians among them, who are living in foreign countries as aliens. For such people, the First Letter of Peter has a direct and poignant relevance; it's addressed to persons such as they are: political exiles and aliens. But most of us live where we are citizens. We are neither exiles nor resident aliens. We do not carry green cards.

Candor requires me to note that the distinguished commentator on the First Letter of Peter, Leonhard Goppelt, interprets the

transferred from one dominion to another, and we become, in whatever culture we find ourselves, resident aliens" (12). The thought is not developed; and I know of no baptismal formula in which such a "transference" of citizenship is even so much as suggested. In baptism one acquires a new, additional citizenship; one does not renounce one's American citizenship, or Canadian citizenship, or whatever.

words as applying to all Christians, everywhere and always. Without even acknowledging the possibility of interpreting them as a literal description of the writer's addressees, namely, Christian members of the Jewish diaspora, he says that the address suggests that Christians "have been set apart from the nations of the world by election and live scattered among them as foreigners who have no homeland here ... [Christians] are living in society as 'diaspora.'"[7]

The closest Goppelt comes to an argument for this interpretation is his remark that "Christians are foreigners among their fellow human beings, even among relatives and acquaintances, because their existence has been established on a totally new basis. They are 'elected' or — as is said subsequently in 1:3 — 'born anew to a living hope through Jesus Christ's resurrection from the dead'" (67). The fact that Christians have been elected to be born anew strikes me as woefully inadequate support for the conclusion that the author of the First Letter of Peter was using the terms "resident aliens" and "exiles" to tell us how Christians in general should think of their political status. The references to the dispersion, to living among Gentiles in Pontus, Galatia, and so on, seem to me decisive evidence against that interpretation. But no matter. Suppose that the writer was not using the terms literally to indicate the political status of his addressees but was instead using them to indicate that Christians in general are elect, born anew by the Spirit. It does not follow that Christians living, say, in present-day America, should regard and comport themselves as if they were resident aliens in the state of which they are citizens.

---

[7] Leonhard Goppelt, *A Commentary on I Peter* (Grand Rapids: Wm. B. Eerdmans Publishing Co., 1993).

The New Testament passage in which Christians in general are clearly described as aliens is Hebrews 11:8–10. The passage opens as follows:

> By faith Abraham obeyed when he was called to go out to a place which he was to receive as an inheritance, and he went out, not knowing where he was to go. By faith he sojourned in the land of promise, as in a foreign land, living in tents with Isaac and Jacob, heirs with him of the same promise. For he looked forward to the city which has foundations, whose builder and maker is God.

Abraham "sojourned in the land of promise, as in a foreign land." He did so because Palestine was for him at the time a foreign land – speaking literally. The promise of the land was still just that, a promise.

Having said that, however, the writer then strikes the note characteristic of the Letter to the Hebrews, that the people of God, wherever they happen to find themselves, whether within the jurisdiction of their own sovereign or as aliens under some other sovereign, look forward to a city of a different order, a city whose builder and maker is not human but divine – the heavenly city. "They desire a better country, that is, a heavenly one" (11:16). All those who live in the faith that God will bring about that heavenly city acknowledge thereby that life on earth has a sort of interim status. Their faith makes "clear that they are seeking a homeland [*patris*]" and that, in that regard, they are "strangers [*xenoi*] and exiles [*parepidemoi*] on the earth" (11:13–14). Earth is a temporary stopping point. But from that it does not follow that either they are aliens in whatever political jurisdiction they find themselves or should regard and comport themselves as if they were aliens.

Polycarp was one of those who looked forward to dwelling in that heavenly city. Smyrna was not that city. Thus Polycarp lived in Smyrna as a sojourner of sorts, a stranger and exile, metaphorically speaking. Yet he regarded himself as a citizen of Smyrna and under the authority of the emperor. He did not regard and comport himself as if he were a stranger and political exile in Smyrna.[8]

---

[8] In Philippians 3:19–20, Paul speaks of those whose "minds are set on earthly things," and then says that "our citizenship [*politeuma*, commonwealth, place of citizenship] is in heaven, and it is from there that we are expecting a Savior, the Lord Jesus Christ." Paul cannot have meant to imply by these words that he did not regard himself as a Roman citizen. In Acts 22:25 we read that, when officials in Jerusalem had seized him and were preparing to scourge him, he said to them, "Is it lawful for you to scourge a man who is a Roman citizen and uncondemned?" Subsequently Paul claimed his rights as a Roman citizen and appealed to Caesar.

CHAPTER 4

Authority

Our project in this essay in political theology is to arrive at an understanding of two dualities: the duality of political authority mediating divine authority, and the duality of Christians being under the authority of both church and state. Having dealt with two major objections to this way of framing the issues, we are now ready to get on with the task.

The state is what I shall call a *governance-authority structure*; the church *has* a governance-authority structure. These are two in a vast panoply of governance-authority structures. In turn, authority to govern extends beyond governance-authority structures, and authority in general extends beyond authority to govern. I propose opening our discussion by saying a bit about these broader phenomena, authority, governance, and authority to govern.

Books have been written about these matters. Here I will do little more than identify the phenomena, my purpose in doing so being that we keep them in mind when we discuss the two dualities. Failure to keep these broader phenomena in mind when discussing the two dualities leads easily to false generalizations. We will come across some examples of such false generalizations in the course of our discussion. In this chapter I will make some remarks about authority in general, in the next, some remarks about governance in general, and in the subsequent chapter, some remarks about authority to govern.[1]

Sometimes we say of a person that he *is an authority* on some topic, or that he *speaks with authority.* This sort of authority, though fundamental to our social existence, is not the sort of authority that we are concerned with here. Our concern is with *having* the authority to *perform some* action. This sort of authority is something one *has,* not something one *is.*[2] When we need a term for this kind of authority, I shall call it *performance-authority.*

If one has the authority to do something, one has the right to do it, "right" being understood as *permission.* As Thomas Hobbes remarks, "by authority, is always understood a right of doing any act" (*Leviathan,* chapter 16). The converse is not the case. Writing this book is something that I am permitted to do; but it would be odd, though perhaps not mistaken, to say that I have the authority to write it. So too, though I am permitted to walk on the Charlottesville Mall, it would be odd to say that I have the authority to do so.

For some purposes it might be important to explore what makes it correct and apt to describe some of the things one is permitted to do as things one has the authority to do but not others; for our purposes here, that is not important. I think this much can be said, however: if the action in question is governance, then if one is permitted to govern someone with respect to certain actions on their part, it is correct and apt to say that one has the authority to do so.

---

[1] In placing my discussion of governmental authority within this larger context I am consciously following in the footsteps of Abraham Kuyper. See especially his chapter "Calvinism and Politics" in his *Calvinism: The Stone Lectures for 1898–1899* (New York: Fleming H. Revell Co., n.d.), pp. 98–142.

[2] In Chapter 7 I will take note of a third concept of authority, namely, *being in a position of authority.*

Sometimes one's authority to do something is the legal authority to do it, the legal right. In other cases one's authority comes along with some social role or position that one has or with some social practice in which one is engaged. But sometimes the right that comes with the authority to do something is the *moral* right to do that thing. Our concern in what follows is exclusively with this last sort of authority; when I speak of someone as having the authority to do something, I mean to imply that he has the moral right to do that thing, that he is morally permitted to do it.

Sometimes, though by no means always, one has the authority to do something because someone has authorized one to do it. The idea of *authorized action* will play an important role in our discussion: God authorizes the state to do certain things. So let's think a bit about this phenomenon of being authorized to do certain things.

Authorized action pervades society. People are authorized to dig holes in certain places, to wear certain kinds of headgear, to enter certain rooms, to sit in certain chairs, to sign certain documents, to issue certain declarations. A judge is authorized to pronounce the defendant *guilty*, an umpire is authorized to declare the batter *out*, a college president is authorized to pronounce the graduating students *bachelors of arts*, a member of the clergy is authorized to pronounce the couple *husband and wife*, the person elected president of the United States is authorized to take up residence in the White House. We are immersed in authorized action.

Authorization to perform some action is acquired in many ways. Sometimes it is acquired by having it conferred on one by someone who himself has the authority to perform that action. When I authorize my attorney to sign some documents on my behalf, I confer on him an authority that I have. So too when the

CEO of an organization authorizes his department heads to make decisions in their areas, he confers on them an authority that he himself has.

Though the examples mentioned are both examples of the conferral of authority to do something that the authorizer himself has the authority to do, they differ in a way that will be important in our subsequent discussion. My attorney acts as my deputy, my proxy. His signing the documents *counts as* my signing the documents; he signs them *on my behalf.* But the decisions of the department heads do not *count as* decisions of the CEO; the department heads are not deputized to act *on behalf of* the head of the operation. The decisions they make are theirs and theirs alone. Rather than being *deputized* to make certain decisions, they are *delegated the authority* to make certain decisions.

Being authorized to take up residence in the White House is different from both of these examples in that it is not conferred by someone who already has the authority to live there. It comes along with being installed in the office of President of the United States. So too, the authorization of clergy to officiate at weddings is not conferred on them (in the United States) by officials who themselves have the authority to officiate at weddings but comes along with their being ordained as clergy.

Yet another way in which one can acquire authorization to perform certain actions is by compact or agreement. A group of us get together to form, say, a chess club. We create a simple organizational structure consisting of the offices of president and treasurer, and we establish a few bylaws. These bylaws declare that the president is authorized to call meetings, they declare that the treasurer is authorized to assess an annual membership fee, and they establish rules whereby the membership can elect one of its members to the office of president and another to the office of treasurer. By being elected to the office of president, a member is then authorized to call meetings, and by being elected to the office of treasurer, a member is authorized to assess an annual membership fee.

Rather than taking note of yet other ways in which one can be authorized to perform actions of a certain sort, let's move on to note the following distinction between two kinds of authorized actions: some actions are such that it is impossible to perform those actions without being authorized to do so whereas others are such that one could in principle perform those actions without being authorized to do so. The action of taking up residence in the White House is an example of the latter sort; one could in principle perform it without being authorized to do so. There would be an outcry if one did; but it can be done. By contrast, the only person who can pronounce a person guilty of a crime is a person authorized to do so, namely, a judge; and in American baseball, the only person who can call a player out is a person authorized to do so, namely, an umpire. Other people may shout "out"; often they do. But only the umpire can call a player out.

Latin has two words that are translated into English as "power," *potentia* and *potestas*. One has the *potentia* to perform some action in case one has the ability to *cause* it to happen – the power to take up residence in the White House, for example. One has the *potestas* to perform some action in case one is able to perform it on account of being authorized to perform it; the ability of an umpire to call the batter out is an example.

This distinction between *potentia* and *potestas* leads to a fundamental point about the nature of authorization. If the only way in which we human beings could do something was by bringing things about causally, nobody could declare someone guilty. More important for our purposes, nobody could be authorized to do anything. Authorization to do something can occur only by way of some other action *counting as* the authorization. Authorization is in that way a *social* fact, not a causal fact. The connection between the act that generates the authorization and the authorization itself is like the connection between the uttering of a sentence and the making of an assertion thereby. The uttering does not *cause* the asserting; it *counts as* the asserting. On other occasions I have delved into the nature of count-generation;[3] for our purposes here that will not be necessary.

Among the sorts of actions that we human beings have the authority to perform is that of governing others – governing certain actions of certain people. Sometimes we have the authority to govern someone by virtue of having been authorized to govern those actions of those people; sometimes we have the authority to do so without anybody ever having authorized us. An example of the latter is the authority of parents to govern their children with respect to certain actions. Just as authority in general pervades society, as does authorization, so also do those specific forms of these which consist of authority to govern and of authorized governance.

---

[3] Most recently in chapter 5 of my *Divine Discourse* (Cambridge University Press, 1995).

Governance

Let us now reflect a bit on why and how governance emerges in human affairs and take note of some of the peculiarities of the sort of governance that states exercise.

There are two fundamentally different sorts of governance. To see the difference, consider the following passage from Yves Simon's *A General Theory of Authority.*[1] Where Simon uses the term "authority," think *governance*.

> What the thinkers opposed to authority generally mean is that authority can never be vindicated except by such deficiencies as are found in children, in the feeble-minded, the emotionally unstable, the criminally inclined, the illiterate, and the historically primitive. The real problem is not whether authority must wither away; no doubt, it will always play an all-important part in human affairs. *The problem is whether deficiencies alone cause authority to be necessary.* It is obvious, indeed, that in many cases the need for authority originates in some defect and disappears when sufficiency is attained. But the commonly associated negation, viz., that authority never originates in the positive qualities of man and society, is by no means obvious and should not be received uncritically. (21–22)

One form that governance of others takes is governance of those who are incapable of forming and carrying out a rational plan of action for themselves, small children and the "feeble-minded"

---

[1] Yves Simon, *A General Theory of Authority* (University of Notre Dame Press, 1980). References are incorporated into the text.

being the best examples. Someone has to govern them in their stead, on their behalf. The other form that governance of others takes is governance of those who are capable of forming and carrying out a rational plan of action. Governance in this case consists of the combination of someone issuing directives to another person and the recipient complying with those directives, the *telos* of this combination being to bring about what is judged to be some good (this good perhaps consisting of averting what is judged to be an evil). It is governance of the latter sort, governance of those who are capable of forming and carrying out a rational plan of action, that is our concern in this essay.

Consider how governance of the latter sort enters and takes form in some organization or institution – a business enterprise, for example. Imagine someone who has decided to make hand-crafted furniture for sale. At first he works by himself. But the business grows; and in order to keep up with demand he hires some craftsmen to help him make the furniture. Now governance sets in. The owner issues directives to his employees and they conform. Sometimes his instructions are specific; "do this," he says to one of the craftsmen, "do that," he says to another. But running the enterprise would be impossible if he confined himself to specific instructions like that; so he issues general rules. Either way, let's call them *directives*. There's more to running the enterprise than governance of the employees; the owner has to keep books, order supplies, and so forth. But governance is central.

Why does governance set in? Because the employees have to work together at producing furniture; and this requires that they agree on the sort of furniture that they will produce – agree on the goal, the end, the *telos* of the enterprise in which they are jointly engaged – and coordinate their contributions to that goal. Sometimes we human beings work together at some project without any governance. Nobody issues directives; we all just see what has to be done and we do it, or we talk it over and come to an agreement, or entrenched habits and practices carry us along. None of these holds for our furniture-making enterprise.

Suppose that the enterprise grows to the point where the owner finds that he can no longer manage it by himself. He then differentiates the management of the enterprise into various positions – treasurer, office manager, and the like – and hires people to fill the positions.

Not all positions in this differentiated management structure will involve governance of the craftsmen; the position of treasurer will not. But most likely some of the positions will involve governance of the craftsmen; the owner will have authorized the persons holding certain management positions to issue directives to the craftsmen. Then, instead of one person governing the work of the craftsmen, there will be a governance structure doing that, this structure consisting of positions, job descriptions attached to the positions, and persons filling the positions.

Those who occupy positions in the management structure, including those who occupy positions that involve governing the work of the craftsmen, are themselves governed by superiors, everybody ultimately being governed by the owner. Until we get to the top, everybody is governed by somebody, including those who are themselves engaged in governance. The enterprise has a multi-level governance structure.

Society as we know it is full of organizations and institutions with such multi-level governance structures. Universities have multi-level governance structures, factories do, hospitals, construction firms, banks. They could not offer the goods or provide the services that they do if they did not. And states are multi-level governance structures.

When speaking of a business enterprise, it's possible and often necessary to distinguish between what the enterprise does *qua* enterprise and what the owner and employees do in the course of carrying out their assignments within the enterprise. The enterprise itself does things by way of human beings who have a position within the enterprise doing things; their doing those things *counts as* the enterprise doing such-and-such. There is no other way in which the enterprise can act. But many of the things people do in their positions within the enterprise do not count as the enterprise doing something. Sometimes it's not clear whether their actions do or do not have that significance.

This distinction applies to all institutions with governance structures, including then the state. The state itself does certain things; and those who hold positions within the state do things. The state declares war; an employee in the post office hands me a sheet of stamps. Some of the actions performed by those in some position within the state count as the state's doing something; some do not. The postal clerk handing me a sheet of stamps does not so count. When such "counting as" does take place, what the state does is different from what the person does (or persons do) whose action(s) counts as the state doing something. A member of the United States Congress cannot declare war; only the state can do that. What a member of Congress can do is vote for declaring war. A majority of the members of Congress voting for a declaration of war counts as the United States government's declaration of war.

Important though it often is to distinguish between what the state does and what someone in some position within the state does, in my discussion I will sometimes ignore the distinction and speak of the state doing something even though the precise thing to say would be that someone in some position within the state did that thing.

States are highly idiosyncratic examples of governance-structures. It's important for our subsequent purposes to take note of two of those idiosyncrasies.

Business enterprises are typically laced through with governance. Certain persons within the enterprise exercise governance over the work of others within the enterprise, others exercise governance over them, and so forth, until we get to the person at the top who exercises governance over all the employees. But governance as exercised by a business enterprise does not extend beyond employees and their work.

That last claim must be qualified. Suppose that our furniture-making enterprise sells its furniture in a store that it owns and operates. And suppose that toward the end of the year it finds that it has a larger inventory than is desirable; so it announces a year-end sale. A mob shows up looking for bargains. Fist-fights break out, some of the furniture is broken. The employees do their best to restore order. It would not be incorrect to say that they do their best to *govern* the behavior of the clients in the store. The governance in this case, however, is at least as much like the governance of someone who is incapable of governing himself as it is like governance that consists of issuing directives and having them obeyed so as to achieve some good.

Now consider my relation to the United States government. I do not hold, and never have held, a position in the United States government. Yet the American state undertakes to govern my activities. It issues directives to me in the form of laws and executive rulings; and it punishes me if it determines that I have not conformed to its directives. It does the same for everyone else within the area of its sovereignty – citizens, visitors, travelers, legal immigrants, illegal immigrants, everybody.

Let me introduce the term "public governance," meaning governance by the state of *the public* – not governance of those who hold positions within the state, which is *internal* governance, but governance of the public. (Those who hold positions in the government are also members of the public and thus subject to public governance.) States do much more than engage in governance; they offer services of various kinds to the public, among the most important of these being that of defending the public against attack by foreign persons or entities. Most of those services require governance internal to the state. But nobody would deny that exercising public governance is central to what the state does.

It's easy to understand why the state exercises internal governance over those who hold positions in the state. It's also easy to understand why it regulates the behavior of those who show up as clients for its services – why it regulates the behavior of those who show up to buy stamps in a post office, for example. But why does the state govern me even though I do not hold a position in the state and even when I am not in or on government property? Why does it govern me all the time, even when I am at home with my family or out on a hike in the wilderness? Why are there no locations within its territory where I can escape its governance?

Very strange. Nothing like it. When the employees of our furniture-making enterprise leave work, they are no longer under the governance of the owner. It must be that some great good is thought to be achieved, or some great evil averted, by the combination of public governance by the state and the members of the public conforming to that governance.

It's not plausible to think that that good is somehow intrinsic to governance and conformity – that these are intrinsically good things. It must be that the combination of the state's public governance and our conforming thereto is *instrumental* to bringing about some great good or averting some great evil. What might that be? What might be the great good that governance of everybody always, coupled with conformity by everybody always, is thought to bring about, or the great evil that is thought to be averted? We'll get to answering this question in Chapter 8.

There's another idiosyncratic feature of the state's governance that should be noted. The state's public governance of those within its territorial jurisdiction is ultimate. Though we all recognize this feature of the state's public governance, it's not easy to state precisely what it comes to. Perhaps the following comes close. When the state issues a directive to the public and someone within the territorial jurisdiction of the state wishes to protest that directive, there is never a procedure for appealing to any institution other than the state itself – unless the state has explicitly surrendered its sovereignty on that matter to some other institution, some international tribunal, for example. So too, when the state makes the decision that someone has not complied with one of its directives to the public there is never a procedure for appealing to any institution other than the state itself – unless, once again, the state has explicitly surrendered its sovereignty on that matter to some other institution. I can protest certain directives issued to me by my university by appealing to the state; I cannot protest directives that my state issues to me as a member of the public by appealing to my university. There is no "higher authority."

It is commonly said that what also distinguishes the state in the modern world is that it has a monopoly on coercive power. That seems to me not true. It has a monopoly on certain forms of coercive power, indeed; but coercion by persons, and by social entities other than the state, pervades society. Social existence would be impossible without it.

CHAPTER 6

Authority to govern

Prominent among the many things that we human beings have the authority to do is the authority to govern actions of our fellow human beings. Having noted how pervasive in our human existence are authority in general and governance in general, let us now look briefly at the combination of the two, authority to govern. One example among many of the authority to govern is the authority of the state to govern the actions of its citizens and of non-citizens within its territorial jurisdiction. Our aim in this chapter is to gain some understanding of the type, authority to govern, before we focus, in subsequent chapters, on that example.[1]

What is authority to govern? The owner of the furniture-making enterprise that we imagined in Chapter 5 has the authority to govern his employees. In what does that authority consist? Let's approach our answer to that question by first considering what it is for the employees to *treat* some directive of the owner as authoritative.

For the employees to treat as authoritative some directive of the owner to perform some action is for them to regard the owner's having directed them to perform that action as generating in them an obligation to perform that action. The employees may believe

---

[1] I give a fuller account than I do here of authority to govern in my essay "Accounting for the Political Authority of the State," in my *Understanding Liberal Democracy*, ed. Terence Cuneo (Oxford University Press, forthcoming).

that they know better than the owner what would be good or right to do; they may think he's making a mistake. Nonetheless, they defer to his enunciated will, allow his enunciated will to direct their will, doing so not just because they think that would be a good thing to do but because they believe that his enunciation of his will has generated in them an obligation to act as directed. More precisely: they defer to his enunciated will unless they believe they have an obligation not to perform the action he is directing them to perform which outweighs the obligation that his enunciated will has generated in them. To treat some directive of the owner as authoritative is to regard it as generating in one a *prima facie* obligation to comply, not necessarily an *ultima facie* obligation.

Deferring to the will of the owner in this way is to be distinguished from deferring to his judgment. The employees may do what the owner directs them to do because they want to do what's best to do and they believe that the owner has a better grip on that than they do. That is not to treat the owner's directive as authoritative but as wise. The former consists of deferring to his enunciated will; the latter, of deferring to his judgment. Treating his directive as authoritative is also different from doing what the owner directs them to do because they are fearful of what will happen to them if they don't. That is not deferring to his enunciated will as authoritative but deferring to his power.

If this is what it is for the employees to treat some directive of the owner as authoritative, what, then, is it for the owner to *have* authority to govern his employees? What is it for him to *possess* that authority? It's for him to be able to issue directives to them that *are authoritative*. Yes; but what is it for him to be able to do that?

What else could it be but that he has the *potestas* and the right, by issuing some directive to them, actually to *generate* in them the (*prima facie*) obligation to do what he directed them to do, to make them *morally bound* to do that. It's to have the *potestas* and the right to issue directives that are *morally binding*. Leslie Green puts it well:

It is of the nature of authority that it purports to impose binding, content-independent reasons for action on its subjects. This fact is usually and properly described as the power of authorities to obligate their subjects. In political contexts, it is evident in the claim that the enactment of a statute creates duties for citizens and officials to behave in certain ways.[2]

For one reason or another the employees may already have been obligated to do what the owner now directs them to do. If so, then whatever the ground of their already being obligated, they now have an additional ground of obligation. John Locke made the point lucidly in his early *Second Tract on Government* (ca. 1662).

[The] obligation of human law can be of two forms: material or formal. (i) A material obligation exists when the thing itself which is the subject-matter of the human law is in itself binding upon the conscience, i.e., it was already fully obligatory by reason of divine law before the human law was passed. (ii) A formal obligation exists when something which is otherwise indifferent is imposed on the people by the authority of a legitimate magistrate, by reason of which imposition it obliges the conscience. Some laws therefore oblige by reason of their content, others by reason only of the magistrate's command.[3]

Locke does not mention that what one became formally obligated to do might be something that one was already materially obligated to do.

Suppose that what the owner directs some employee to do is not something that he was already obligated to do but something that

[2] Leslie Green, *The Authority of the State* (Oxford University Press, 1988), p. 127.
[3] *John Locke: Political Writings*, ed. David Wooton (Indianapolis: Hackett Publishing Co., 1993), p. 175.

he was already obligated *not* to do. Is that employee then faced with a conflict of obligations? Has that directive turned what was previously an *ultima facie* obligation not to do that thing into what is now only a *prima facie* obligation, possibly outweighed in its normative force by the normative force of the directive?

It has not. In such a case, the owner lacks the *potestas* to generate in the employee the obligation to do as he directed. The owner may direct some sentences in the imperative mood at the employee. But if the employee is morally obligated not to do X, then the owner cannot, by uttering those sentences, make him obligated to do X. The situation is not that the owner *can and does* generate in the employee the (*prima facie*) obligation to do X but does not have the *right* to do so, and hence *ought not* to do so. The situation is rather that the owner lacks the *potestas* to bind the employee in this way. The directive he issues is not authoritative because it's not morally binding. Recall that we are talking throughout about moral authority, not about legal authority or the authority that comes along with some role that one occupies.

Suppose that the owner directs some employee to do something that the employee is morally permitted to do but that the owner is not morally permitted to direct him to do – perhaps to submit peacefully to some harsh and arbitrary treatment. Would such a command generate in the employee the obligation to obey? I think not. Here too the situation is not that by issuing the directive the owner can and does generate the obligation but that he had no right to do that; the situation is rather that he lacks the *potestas* to generate an obligation in the employee by issuing the directive. A condition of having the *potestas* to issue a binding directive to someone to do something is that it be morally permissible to direct him to do that. This principle applies not only to the sort of case imagined in this paragraph but also to the sort of case imagined in the preceding paragraph, since a condition of its being morally permissible to direct someone to do something is that it's not something that he is obligated not to do.

An essay that enjoys near-classic status in contemporary discussions concerning political authority is Richard B. Friedman's "On the Concept of Authority in Political Philosophy." In the essay Friedman observes that

> it is now commonplace in political philosophy as well as in social science to assume that the notion of authority belongs to a network of concepts having to do with the various ways in which some men get other men to do what they wish, such as power, domination, coercion, force, manipulation, persuasion, etc. Authority thus appears as a species of the genus "social control" or "influence" and hence as a concept coordinate with yet distinct from, say, coercion or persuasion through rational argument. From this perspective, then, an account of the nature of authority must be cast in the form of an exploration of the relation between authority and the other notions forming this network of influence-terms, and the main task of analysis thus becomes that of exhibiting the distinctive type of influence involved in the idea of authority.[4]

I have set my discussion of the authority to govern in the context of the authority to do things – performance-authority I called it – rather than in the context of ways of exerting influence over people. Why do political philosophers and social scientists typically think of authority to govern as a species of influence rather than as a species of the authority, and hence the right, to do something? Why do they typically locate the concept of authority within the "network of influence-terms" rather than within the network of normative concepts?

---

[4] Richard B. Friedman, "On the Concept of Authority in Political Philosophy," reprinted in Richard E. Flathman, ed., *Concepts in Social & Political Philosophy* (New York: Macmillan Publishing Co., 1973), pp. 121–46.

Part of the answer is that though they typically describe their topic as authority, it is, in fact, not authority in general that is their concern but only authority to govern; had their concern been performance-authority in general, locating the concept of authority within the network of influence-terms would have had no plausibility whatsoever. Having the authority to wear a certain kind of headgear in a procession is not a case of exerting influence over someone. I referred in the previous chapter to Yves Simon's book *A General Theory of Authority*. The only type of performance-authority that Simon takes note of is authority to govern. His theory is thus far from being a *general* theory of performance-authority. I have no explanation for why it is that he and others fail to note that authority to govern is just one species of authority to do something.

The fact that discussions labeled as discussions of authority are almost always only about authority to govern is not sufficient, however, to account for the fact that those discussions typically locate authority within the network of influence-terms. In the essay mentioned above, Friedman distinguishes *de jure* authority from *de facto* authority and remarks that it is the *de facto* concept that he and most other philosophers and social scientists have their eye on when discussing authority. This explains why they think of authority to govern as a species of influence.

The explanation of authority to govern that I offered above was an explanation of *de jure* authority. Someone may have *de jure* authority over me but refrain from exercising his authority, perhaps because I am already doing what he wants me to do and what he has the authority to direct me to do; in such a case, I do not conform to his directives and he does not exert influence over me. Or he may both possess and exercise his *de jure* authority to issue directives to me but I may think that he does not have the authority to do this and may refuse, on that ground, to conform;

once again, he does not exert influence over me. Or I may acknowledge that he does have *de jure* authority to issue directives to me but, out of laziness, stubbornness, resentment, cowardice, or whatever, may fail or refuse to do what he directs me to do; in this way too he can possess and exercise *de jure* authority to issue directives to me without exerting influence over me. Had political philosophers and social scientists been working with the concept of *de jure* authority, thinking of authority as a species of influence would have had no plausibility whatsoever.

One has *de facto* authority over someone just in case the recipient treats one's directives as authoritative; one may or may not also have *de jure* authority over him. Having *de facto* authority over someone is, by definition, a mode of exerting influence over him.

Is it a matter of preference whether we use the *de jure* or the *de facto* concept when discussing authority to govern? It is not. The concept we need for our purposes is the *de jure* concept. Our topic is the relation between the authority of the state and God's authority. We cannot arrive at an understanding of that relation by discussing the relation between *treating* the directives of the state as authoritative and *treating* God's commands as authoritative.

Let's pull things together: by the "political authority" of the state I mean the *de jure* authority of the state to govern the public. A legitimate state has the authority to do many more things than exercise governance of the public. It has the authority to exercise internal governance over its employees, the authority to declare war, the authority to make international treaties, the authority to pronounce certain people *guilty* of a crime, and so forth. But the exercise of political authority is central to the task of the state.

CHAPTER 7

Calvin on God, governmental authority, and obedience

Having set the context for our discussion by looking at authority in general, at governance in general, and at authority to govern in general, we are now ready to embark on the project of developing a political theology at the center of which is an account of the two dualities, the duality of the political authority of the state mediating divine authority and the duality of Christians being under the authority of both church and state.

Political authority is extraordinary. Are we sure that the state has such authority, that is, *de jure* authority to govern the public by issuing directives to them that are binding? If the state does have such authority, how did it come by it? Most writers on these matters, both in the past and in the present, assume that legitimate states do have political authority.[1] The standard pre-modern account of such authority was that states have such authority by virtue of divine authorization: God bestows such authority on the state. Hobbes and Locke initiated what Lilla calls "the great

---

[1] Given how most writers understand the concept of legitimacy, this may well be for them a conceptual truth. But suppose someone holds that the directives that states issue do not have binding authority; they do not generate in the public an obligation to obey. Usually it's prudent to conform. The thing one does in conforming may be a good thing to do, maybe even obligatory. But the state's directing one to do it does not generate in one the obligation to do it. It seems to me that someone who holds this position is not thereby forced to hold that the concept of legitimacy is inapplicable to states; he might instead argue for a different understanding of that concept from the customary understanding.

separation" from the tradition by developing accounts of political authority from below rather than from above. Most subsequent writers on political authority have followed them in that. Lilla remarks that when you and I now look at attempts from above, we have the sense of gazing at a distant shore.[2]

Suppose that one or another of the attempts to account for political authority from below is successful. Does that mean that discussing the relation between divine authority and political authority has lost its point? Would the success of some account from below sound the death knell to this part of political theology? Before we proceed further, must we establish that all extant attempts to account for political authority from below have failed and that there is good reason to think that all future attempts will fail as well?[3]

The answer to these questions is No. It's probably true that the emergence of attempts to account for political authority from below contributed historically to the decline of political theology. But there is no necessary connection. God may authorize the state to do what it also has the authority to do for some other reason. In fact I judge this to be the case.[4] But rather than elaborating that point here, let's return to it at the end of the next chapter, after we have developed an account of the relation between divine authority and political authority. We can then see more clearly why an

---

[2] Mark Lilla, *The Stillborn God: Religion, Politics, and the Modern West* (New York: Vintage Books, 2008), p. 4.

[3] The most substantial recent discussions of political authority are the following: Margaret Gilbert, *A Theory of Political Obligation* (Oxford: Clarendon Press, 1988); Leslie Green, *The Authority of the State* (Oxford University Press, 1988); George Klosko, *Political Obligations* (Oxford University Press, 2005); and A. John Simmons, *Moral Principles and Political Obligations* (Princeton University Press, 1979).

[4] In my essay "Accounting for the Political Authority of the State," in my *Understanding Liberal Democracy*, ed. Terence Cuneo (Oxford University Press, forthcoming), I develop an account from below of political authority.

account of political authority from below does not render pointless an account from above.

The Christian scriptures, both Old Testament and New, have much to say about the relation between God and political authority; and pre-modern theologians and political theorists appealed to a wide range of these passages in developing their position. Far and away the most influential passage was the first seven verses of chapter 13 of Paul's letter to the Romans. Christians under persecution have often employed the image of the great beast, found in Revelation 13, to describe the tyrannous regime under which they found themselves. But Romans 13 is the *locus classicus* for Christian views of the state. The first two verses are these:

Let every person be subject to the governing authorities. For there is no authority except from God, and those that exist have been instituted by God. Therefore he who resists the authorities resists what God has appointed, and those who resist will incur judgment.

In *Moral Principles and Political Obligations*, the philosopher A. John Simmons quotes these verses and then, referring to the pre-modern period, remarks that

The doctrine of St. Paul was nearly universally accepted by political theorist and layman alike ... The political authority of kings was believed to be granted by God, and the duties of citizens toward their king were imposed by God. Neither the conduct of kings nor the behavior of individual citizens played any part in the generation of political bonds or authority. It was in reaction to this view, and the passive and unconditional obedience by the citizen which it commanded, that consent theory and the corresponding doctrine of political authority arose, amid the unrest and rebellion of the seventeenth and eighteenth centuries.[5]

---

[5] Simmons, *Moral Principles and Political Obligations*, pp. 58–59.

Simmons here assumes that Paul did teach that citizens are to render passive and unconditional obedience to government; he calls this "the doctrine of St. Paul." I will argue in the next chapter that this is not what Paul taught. But Simmons is correct in saying that this is how Paul was traditionally interpreted. So before tackling Romans for ourselves in the next chapter, I propose having before us what arguably became the most influential of all traditional interpretations, that by John Calvin in the final chapter of his *Institutes*.[6] Calvin cites an astoundingly wide range of biblical passages in support of his view. But the main outlines of his view are presented as an interpretation of Paul in Romans.

In my presentation of Calvin's view I will do more quoting, and less paraphrasing and summarizing, than commentators usually do. I have three reasons for this. Calvin's views on these matters became so influential that I think we should have those views before us in translations of the very words that proved influential. Second, a good deal of what Calvin says is so astounding to us, as it was to many of his contemporaries, that the reader needs to be assured that what is being attributed to Calvin was indeed Calvin's view and is not a contestable interpretation thereof. And third, Calvin's rhetoric in this final chapter of the *Institutes* is extraordinarily lucid and vivid.[7]

Calvin found many of the views about civil government expressed in his day to be appalling; the presentation of his own view is, accordingly, highly polemical. On one side are those who "strive to overturn this divinely established order"; on the other side are "the flatterers of princes, immoderately praising their

---

[6] Luther's interpretation became very nearly as influential as Calvin's.

[7] I am using the translation by Ford Lewis Battles, *Institutes of the Christian Religion* (Philadelphia: Westminster Press, 1950). References are incorporated into the text.

power." "Unless both these evils are checked, purity of faith will perish" (IV.xx.1).

"Man is under a twofold government [*duplex in homine regimen*]," says Calvin, spiritual and civil. Calvin's topic is the latter; and his aim is to show "how lovingly God has provided for humankind" in establishing civil government (IV.xx.1). "It has not come about by human perversity that the authority over all things on earth is in the hands of kings and other rulers, but by divine providence and holy ordinance" (IV.xx.4).

Calvin leads off by stating "the appointed end" of civil government. He does so at a number of other places in the chapter as well, with rather wide variations in detail and comprehensiveness. In one place he says that the end is "to provide for the common safety and peace of all" (IV.xx.9). In another place he says that the end is "to preserve the tranquility of [the ruler's] dominion, to restrain the seditious stirrings of restless men, to help those forcibly oppressed, to punish evil deeds" (IV.xx.11). His initial statement is among the most comprehensive:

civil government has as its appointed end, so long as we live among men, to cherish and protect the outward worship of God, to defend sound doctrine of piety and the position of the church, to adjust our life to the society of men, to form our social behavior to civil righteousness, to reconcile us with one another, and to promote general peace and tranquility. (IV.xx.2)[8]

---

[8] The most comprehensive of all is the following: civil government "does not merely see to it . . . that men breathe, eat, drink, and are kept warm, even though it surely embraces all these activities when it provides for their living together. It does not, I repeat, look to this only, but also prevents idolatry, sacrilege against God's name, blasphemies against his truth, and other public offenses against religion from arising and spreading among the people; it prevents the public peace from being disturbed; it provides that each man may keep his property safe and sound; that men may carry on blameless intercourse among themselves; that honesty and modesty may be preserved among men. In short, it provides that a public manifestation of religion may exist among Christians, and that humanity be maintained among men" (IV.xx.3).

That this end may be achieved, magistrates "have a mandate from God, have been invested with divine authority, and are wholly God's representatives, in a manner acting as his vicegerents" (IV. xx.4). "They have been ordained ministers of divine justice"; they are "vicars of God," "deputies of God" (IV.xx.6). Theirs is a "holy ministry"; they are all "ordained by God" (IV.xx.7). "The magistrate in administering punishments does nothing by himself but carries out the very judgments of God"; "all things [done by magistrates] are done on the authority of God" (IV.xx.10).[9]

It follows, says Calvin, that subjects have two fundamental duties toward their magistrates. The first "is to think most honorably of their office, which they [the subjects] recognize as a jurisdiction bestowed by God, and on that account to esteem and reverence them as ministers and representatives of God." Calvin makes a point of adding that he is "not discussing the persons themselves, as if a mask of dignity covered foolishness, or sloth, or cruelty, as well as wicked morals full of infamous deeds." It is not the persons as such but the persons *qua* office-holders who are to receive "honor and reverence"; they are to "receive reverence out of respect for their lordship." We are not just to buckle under to them out of fear but to honor them as God-ordained officials (IV.xx.22).

The second duty is obedience. "With hearts inclined to reverence their rulers, the subjects should prove their obedience toward them, whether by obeying their proclamations, or by paying taxes, or by undertaking public offices and burdens which pertain to the common defense, or by executing any other commands of theirs." For "the magistrate cannot be resisted without God being resisted at the same time" (IV.xx.23). This is true for both the just and the

---

[9] By "magistrate" Calvin sometimes has in mind a particular position within the French government of the time. Usually, however, he uses it to refer to civil authorities in general.

unjust magistrate. "We are not only subject to the authority of princes who perform their office toward us uprightly and faithfully, as they ought, but also to the authority of all who, by whatever means, have got control of affairs, even though they perform not a whit of the prince's office" (IV.xx.25).

Several times over and with great emphasis Calvin makes this point about reverence and obedience.

In a very wicked man utterly unworthy of all honor, provided he has the public power in his hands, that noble and divine power resides which the Lord has by his Word given to the ministers of his justice and judgment. Accordingly, he should be held in the same reverence and esteem by his subjects, in so far as public obedience is concerned, in which they would hold the best of kings if he were given to them. (IV.xx.25)

If we have continually present to our minds and before our eyes the fact that even the most worthless kings are appointed by the same decree by which the authority of all kings is established, those seditious thoughts will never enter our minds that a king should be treated according to his merits, and that it is unfair that we should show ourselves subjects to him who, on his part, does not show himself a king to us. (IV.xx.27)

"We should learn not to examine the men themselves, but take it as enough that they bear, by the Lord's will, a character upon which he has imprinted and engraved an inviolable majesty" (IV.xx.29).

In the final section of the chapter Calvin allows one, and only one, exception to this sweeping injunction to obedience. Obedience to magistrates "is never to lead us away from obedience to [God] ... If they command anything against him, let it go unesteemed" (IV.xx.32). Calvin does not develop the point, and he cites only a few biblical passages in support. He says that we should be willing to "suffer anything rather than turn aside from piety"; we can infer that he would approve Polycarp's refusal to obey the proconsul by renouncing Christ.

In two of his commentaries on biblical books Calvin clarifies his thinking on this point. In his *Lectures on Daniel* (6:22) he says that "when princes forbid the service and worship of God, when they command their subjects to pollute themselves with idolatry and want them to consent to and participate in all the abominations that are contrary to the service of God, they are not worthy to be regarded as princes or to have any authority attributed to them." The idea is clear: when princes act in the ways mentioned, they do not merely do what they ought not to do; they exceed their authority. Hence obedience is not required. Calvin makes the same point in his *Commentary on Acts* (5:29): "If a king, ruler, or magistrate, become so lofty that he diminishes the honor and authority of God, he becomes a mere man."[10]

What does Calvin mean to include under the exception? The examples he mentions are all cases of the magistrate ordering citizens to violate the so-called First Table of the Decalogue.[11] But what if the magistrate does not order me to repudiate God or Christ, does not order me to worship an idol, does not order me to do anything of that sort, but instead orders me to treat my neighbor in a way that God forbids? Am I to disobey?

I am not aware of any passage in which Calvin raises the question. One would think that the principle "If they command anything against [God], let it go unesteemed" applies to these cases as well. But if so, why are Calvin's examples of the exception all cases of the magistrate ordering violations of the First Table?

---

[10] I owe these references to Calvin's commentaries to John Witte's discussion in chapter 1 of his *The Reformation of Rights: Law, Religion, and Human Rights in Early Modern Calvinism* (Cambridge University Press, 2007).

[11] Witte, ibid., pp. 115–16, surveys a large number of passages in which Calvin makes the exception; they are all of this same sort.

What Calvin did clearly hold is that if the magistrate is wronging me, rather than commanding me to wrong one of my fellows, I must submit. His language on the matter is strong:

> If we are cruelly tormented by a savage prince, if we are greedily despoiled by one who is avaricious or wanton, if we are neglected by a slothful one, if finally we are vexed for piety's sake by one who is impious and sacrilegious, let us first be mindful of our own misdeeds, which without doubt are chastised by such whips of the Lord ... Let us then call this thought to mind, that it is not for us to remedy such evils; that only this remains, to implore the Lord's help, in whose hand are the hearts of kings, and the changing of kingdoms. (IV.xx.29)

I find this last point not only troubling but incoherent. Several times over Calvin makes the point, hinted at in this last passage, that oppressive or incompetent rulers should be interpreted as God's punishment of the people for their wrongdoing. Those "who rule unjustly and incompetently have been raised up by him to punish the wickedness of the people" (IV.xx.25). But if being under the thumb of a tyrannical ruler is God's way of punishing us for our wickedness, why would it be appropriate to "implore" God to deliver us? Should we not patiently accept our oppression as the punishment that we've got coming to us?

Three final points of exposition. What Calvin has said thus far concerning patient acceptance of unjust rulers pertains to private individuals. When it comes to the "lower magistrates," something different has to be said. "If there are magistrates of the people, appointed to restrain the willfulness of kings" (IV.xx.31), it is their duty to try to do so, Calvin says:

> I am so far from forbidding them to withstand, in accordance with their duty, the fierce licentiousness of kings that, if they wink at kings who violently fall upon and assault the lowly common folk, I declare that their dissimulation involves nefarious perfidy, because they dishonestly betray

the freedom of the people, of which they know that they have been appointed protectors by God's ordinance. (IV.xx.31)[12]

If there are no lower magistrates, or if the lower magistrates are as corrupt as the king, then it is to God alone that we can address our call for deliverance.

The application of this doctrine of resistance to you and me as citizens of liberal democracies is somewhat different from its application to the subjects of the monarchies of Calvin's day. We are citizens, not subjects. Therefore, some of the responsibilities belonging to the lesser magistrates of Calvin's day belong to us. We must use our rights as citizens, centrally, our right to the ballot box, to "restrain the willfulness" of those who govern us. On Calvin's view we do not, however, have the right to engage in civil disobedience or armed resistance, nor is there any office in a liberal democracy to which that latter right is attached. We are obligated in all things to obey.

Second, in earlier chapters of the *Institutes* Calvin delineated the jurisdiction of the state vis-à-vis that of the church. Though Calvin does not make a point of it in his discussion of civil government in *Institutes*, IV.xx, he no doubt wants us to keep in mind that the jurisdiction of the state is limited by that of the church, as is that of the church by that of the state.

Third, Calvin briefly considers the argument that since "God forbids all Christians to kill," it is impermissible for a Christian to occupy any position in the government that involves killing, whether in warfare, by the imposition of capital punishment, or whatever. "How can magistrates be pious men and shedders of

---

[12] As examples from ancient times of "magistrates of the people" resisting tyranny, Calvin cites the ephors against the Spartan kings, the tribunes of the people against the Roman consuls, and the demarchs against the senate of the Athenians (IV.xx.31).

blood at the same time?" (IV.xx.10). Calvin's answer is that though one may indeed not kill when acting as a private person, when acting in some governmental capacity one may sometimes kill; sometimes one is obligated to do so. In so doing one is acting on God's behalf and at God's command.

> If we understand that the magistrate in administering punishments does nothing by himself, but carries out the very judgments of God, we shall not be hampered by this scruple. The law of the Lord forbids killing; but, that murders may not go unpunished, the Lawgiver himself puts into the hands of his ministers a sword to be drawn against all murderers. It is not for the pious to afflict and hurt; yet to avenge, at the Lord's command the afflictions of the pious is not to hurt or to afflict. Would that this were ever before our minds – that nothing is done here from men's rashness, but all things are done on the authority of God who commands it. (IV.xx.10)

Let us now stand back and reflect critically on what Calvin has said. It will help if I first formulate what he has said as an argument or line of thought which leads to the conclusion that we are obligated to obey the state. Calvin holds that the main points in this argument are taught by Paul in Romans 13 and supported by a large number of other biblical passages.

(1) Anyone who holds a public governance position in civil government does so by virtue of God's providential governance of humankind.

(2) Anyone who holds a public governance position in civil government is in a position of authority.

(3) If someone is in a position of authority in civil government, then, for any directive that falls within his jurisdiction, he has the authority and the right to issue that directive – with the exception of directives that enjoin subjects to violate the First Table of the Decalogue.

(4) Anyone in a position of authority in civil government is functioning as God's deputy (vicar, vicegerent, representative) when he issues directives that he has the authority to issue.

(5) If someone is functioning as God's deputy in issuing a directive, then, by his commanding that so-and-so be done, God commands that that be done.

(6) We are all always obligated to do what God commands.

So far as I can see, the only way to understand why this line of thought seemed plausible to Calvin and to so many others is to conclude that he was running together two distinct concepts of authority.

One of these is the concept analyzed in Chapter 6, *having the authority to govern*, this being understood as a species of *performance-authority*, that is, a species of *having the authority to do something*. In our discussion of performance-authority in general (Chapter 4) I noted that having the authority to do something implies having the right to do it – the *permission*-right. Depending on the case, this right might be a legal right, a right that comes along with some role that one occupies, or a moral right. In this essay our concern is exclusively with performance-authority that carries the last of these sorts of rights. Whenever I say that someone has the authority to do something, I mean to imply that he has the *moral right* to do it. One might say that he has the *moral authority* to do it. In Chapter 6 we saw that to have the authority to govern someone is have the *potestas* to issue directives to him that bind him – directives that generate in him the obligation to act as directed. And we saw that a condition of one's directive being morally binding on someone is that it be morally permissible for one to direct him to do that.

The other concept of authority that Calvin was working with is that of *being in a position of authority*, that is, occupying an institutional position that authorizes one to issue directives to others. Call such authority *positional authority*.[13] What comes along with being in an institutional position of authority is always a certain jurisdiction. By virtue of being in that position of authority, one is authorized to issue directives to certain people on certain matters – not to other people and not to these people on other matters. If one is in an institutional position of authority and the directive that one issues falls within one's jurisdiction, then one has positional authority to issue it even though it might not be morally permissible to do so. But as we have seen, if it is not morally permissible, then it does not generate in the subject an obligation to act as directed.

The clue that Calvin is working with the concept of positional authority is that, on his view, the fact that the magistrate morally ought not to issue some directive does not imply that he lacks authority to do so. What makes sense of the otherwise inexplicable combination in Calvin of stinging rebukes of magistrates for issuing directives that they ought not to issue, with firm injunctions to the public to do whatever the magistrates direct them to do – provided their directives do not fall outside their jurisdiction – is that he is also working with the concept of performance-authority and running the two concepts together.

The magistrates are morally obligated to pursue "the appointed end" of civil government. They are to remember that they are vicars of God, assigned to "watch with all care, earnestness, and diligence, to represent in themselves to men some image of divine providence, protection, goodness, benevolence, and justice. And they should perpetually set before themselves the thought that

---

[13] I borrow the term "positional" from Simmons in his book *Moral Principles and Political Obligations*. I use it somewhat differently from how he uses it, however.

[those are] gravely cursed . . . who deceitfully conduct themselves in a righteous calling" (IV.xx.6). But no matter how "gravely cursed" they may be for the reprehensible way in which they exercise their task, citizens are morally obligated to obey them, provided their directives do not fall outside their jurisdiction, because they are in a position of authority over the citizens.

This is confused. There's no problem with the concept of positional authority as such. There is in fact the phenomenon of being in an institutional position of authority. But consider the case of someone who issues a directive that he has the positional authority to issue but not the moral authority to issue. Such a directive generates in the recipient no obligation to obey; the directive in such a case is not binding. Binding directives correlate with performance-authority, not with positional authority. The reason why Calvin's line of thought seemed plausible to him, so I suggest, is that, while mainly working with the positional concept of authority, when it came to whether or not we have an obligation to obey the government he thought in terms of performance-authority. Run the two concepts together in the way in which he did and his line of thought seems plausible.

An interpretive question that these comments suggest is that of how Calvin should be understood when he says that citizens have no obligation to obey the magistrate if he orders them to violate the First Table of the Decalogue. Should Calvin be understood as saying that the magistrate is exceeding the jurisdiction of his positional authority, or should he be understood as setting the concept of positional authority off to the side and working, at this point, with the concept of the moral authority to do something? Almost certainly in the former way, which is how I interpreted him earlier. He says that the magistrate in such a case becomes a "mere man"; this strongly suggests that he exceeds the jurisdiction of the institutional position of authority that he occupies.

The story has often been told of how the Huguenot refugees and Marian exiles in Geneva during Calvin's lifetime found his doctrine of political authority and obedience intolerable, and how his followers, despite the veneration they felt for the master, struggled to work out an alternative.[14] Milton, writing several generations later, was among the most radical of these.

While also employing the concept of positional authority in his interpretation of the first two verses of Romans 13, Milton struggled to avoid the oppressive conclusions that Calvin drew. In his comments on Romans 13 in the *First Defence* he says this: "Whoever resists authority, that is, lawful authority, resists the ordinance of God. This decree touches kings too, who resist the laws and the senate. But does he who resists an illegitimate authority, or the corrupter and subverter of a legitimate one, resist the ordinance of God? ... The apostle here speaks only of legitimate authority."[15] Milton here attempts to avoid Calvin's conclusions by making two moves that Calvin did not make. First, he distinguishes between a person legitimately occupying some position of authority and a person illegitimately doing so; only the former person occupies his position by virtue of the ordinance of God. And second, he says that those who become corrupters and subverters no longer legitimately occupy their position of authority even if they once did so. Making these two moves amounts to combining, in a certain way, the concept of positional authority with the concept of having the moral authority to do something. If someone who has come to occupy some position of authority by legitimate means then does things that he lacks the moral authority to do, he thereby loses his positional authority; he is no longer in a

<hr>

[14] The most recent telling of the story is that by Witte in *The Reformation of Rights*.

[15] I owe my reference to these passages from Milton to Warren Chernaik, "Biblical Republicanism," *Prose Studies*, 23:1 (April 2000), 147–60.

position of authority. And having lost his positional authority, he can no longer make commands that are ordinances of God. Here is how the passage from *First Defence* continues:

Without magistrates and civil government there can be no state or human society or life itself. But whatever power or magistrate acts in the contrary manner is not truly ordained of God, and therefore we are not obliged or instructed to obey such a power or magistrate, nor debarred from wise opposition, inasmuch as we shall not be resisting the power or the magistrate here favorably depicted, but a cut-purse, a tyrant, and a foe; and if he must be termed magistrate because he has power and may seem appointed by God for our punishment, then by such reasoning the devil himself will be a magistrate.

What Milton does, in effect, is to take the ordinary concept of being in an institutional position of authority and then claim that there are very different conditions attached to occupying an institutional position of authority from those the institutions themselves typically attach; there are moral conditions attached. The law of the land may define the position of king in such a way that even though the decree the king issued was quite horrible, he nonetheless did not exceed his authority when issuing it. Milton says that if this is what the law of the land says, it is mistaken. Since the king morally ought not to have issued the decree, he has exceeded his authority and is no longer in a position of authority.

This is to join Calvin in confusing the two concepts of performance-authority and positional authority, though in a way different from the way Calvin confuses them. In general it's not true, of those who occupy some institutional position of authority, that they exceed their positional authority whenever they issue a decree that they were morally obligated not to issue. They exceed their moral performance-authority, but not their positional authority.

CHAPTER 8

What did Paul actually say?

I observed in the preceding chapter that most Christian theological accounts of the duality of state authority mediating divine authority are based mainly on an interpretation of Romans 13; that will be true of my account as well. So let us now turn to Paul's letter to the church at Rome.

Though some of what Paul says here has implications for the other duality, that of Christians being under the jurisdiction of both church and state, that duality is not his main topic in Romans; we will be discussing that duality in Chapter 11. This present chapter and Chapter 11 thus together constitute the core of our account of the two dualities. The other chapters flesh out the account, pursue some implications, argue against some alternatives, develop other aspects of political theology, and so forth.

It was not obvious to the early Christians how they should comport themselves with respect to the social structures and institutions of their day – family structures, household slave economies, the Roman Empire, and so forth. In the thirteenth chapter of his letter to the Christians in Rome, Paul gave advice to his readers on that last point. The advice was not novel. It was essentially an adaptation to the Roman Empire of what the Old Testament said about the task of the state. I will return to this point after we have learned what advice it was that Paul gave.

Here is the relevant passage in its entirety (New Revised Standard Version translation), prefaced with some verses from the latter half of chapter 12.

[9] Let love be genuine, hate what is evil, hold fast to what is good; love one another with mutual affection ... [14] Bless those who persecute you, bless and do not curse them ... [17] Do not repay anyone evil for evil, but take thought for what is noble in the sight of all. [18] If it is possible, so far as it depends on you, live peaceably with all. [19] Beloved, never avenge [*ekdikeo*] yourselves, but leave room for the wrath [*orgé*] of God; for it is written, "Vengeance [*ekdikēsis*] is mine, I will repay, says the Lord." [20] No, "if your enemies are hungry, feed them; if they are thirsty, give them something to drink, for by doing this you will heap burning coals on their heads." [21] Do not be overcome by evil, but overcome evil with good.

[1] Let every person be subject to the governing authorities [*exousiai*], for there is no authority except from God, and those authorities that exist have been instituted [*tetagmenai*] by God. [2] Therefore whoever resists authority resists what God has appointed, and those who resist will incur judgment [*krima*]. [3] For rulers are not a terror [*phobos*] to good conduct, but to bad. Do you wish to have no fear [verbal form of *phobos*] of the authority? Then do what is good, and you will receive its approval; [4] for it is God's servant [*diakonos*] for your good. But if you do what is wrong, you should be afraid, for the authority does not bear the sword in vain! It is the servant [*diakonos*] of God to execute wrath [*orgé*] on the wrongdoer. [5] Therefore one must be subject, not only because of wrath but also because of conscience. [6] For the same reason you also pay taxes, for the authorities are God's servants [*leitourgoi*] busy with this very thing. [7] Pay to all what is due them – taxes to whom taxes are due, revenue to whom revenue is due, respect to whom respect is due, honor to whom honor is due.

It is not evident how Paul's teaching in chapter 13 fits with what he has just said in chapter 12. Most traditional interpretations, of which Calvin's is an example, hold that in chapter 12 Paul says that whereas believers are not to avenge themselves, God does exercise vengeance (retribution, pay-back); in chapter 13 he then says that God assigns the state the task of exercising vengeance on God's behalf. The way these two points fit together, so it is commonly said, is that in chapter 12 Paul is telling his readers how they are to conduct themselves as individuals whereas in chapter 13 he is talking about official actions of the state. The state is to exercise vengeance (retribution) on God's behalf; individual believers are not to avenge themselves but instead to return evil with good.

This leaves open the question of whether it is permissible for believers to occupy positions in government where their actions count as the government exercising vengeance (retribution). The Catholic, Orthodox, Lutheran, and Reformed traditions have by and large said that this is permissible; the Anabaptist tradition has quite uniformly said that it is not.

If this traditional interpretation is the best we can do, then so be it. But it has a strike against it from the start. Elsewhere I have noted that Jesus often presented his ethic of love in the context of a polemical attack on what I call the *reciprocity code*.[1] The reciprocity code said that good is to be reciprocated with good and evil with evil. Jesus' attitude toward the positive side of the code was that, though it's not a bad rule to follow most of the time, we should gladly do good even to those who cannot reciprocate. His attitude toward the negative side of the code was flat-out rejection. "Love your enemies, do good to those who hate you, bless those who curse you, pray for those who abuse you" (Luke 6:27–28). Paul repeats this teaching of Jesus in Romans 12.[2]

---

[1] See chapter 11 of my *Justice in Love* (Grand Rapids: Wm. B. Eerdmans Publishing Co., 2011).

[2] He also repeats it in 1 Thessalonians: "See that none of you repays evil for evil, but always seek to do good to one another and to all" (5:15). It is also repeated in 1 Peter 3:9: "Do not repay evil for evil or abuse for abuse, but, on the contrary, repay with a blessing."

The core idea of retribution is paying back evil with evil, redressing the harm done to the victim with an equivalent harm done to the wrongdoer. Jesus' rejection of the reciprocity code implies his rejection of retribution — of paying back, of getting even, of avenging, of redressing harm with harm, of returning evil for evil. If hard treatment is to be imposed on the wrongdoer, let it be for the sake of achieving some good in his life and/or the lives of others.

Should we understand Jesus as allowing for an exception? Should we understand him as meaning that though individual persons must reject the reciprocity code and live instead by the ethic of love, the state need not do so; it may exercise retribution? Nowhere does Jesus even hint at such an exception. Those who hold that Jesus should be understood as tacitly allowing for it bear the burden of proof, as do those who think that Paul meant to allow for this exception.[3]

We need not ask whether the burden can be borne. For the assumption underlying the traditional interpretation — that Paul says that God assigns the state to do what individual believers are forbidden to do — is mistaken. In chapter 12 Paul uses the Greek word *ekdikêsis*, which is translated in our English Bibles as "vengeance." The word "*ekdikêsis*" occurs nowhere in chapter 13. Paul does not say that God has assigned government the task of exercising *ekdikêsis* — the task of exercising vengeance or retribution, of repaying evil with evil, of redressing harm with harm. He says that God has assigned government the task of executing wrath or anger at wrongdoers. Executing wrath or anger at wrongdoers need not take the form of repaying evil with

---

[3] I will be coming back later to how we should interpret 12:19: "Beloved, never avenge yourselves, but leave room for the wrath of God; for it is written, 'Vengeance is mine, I will repay, says the Lord.'"

evil; it may instead take the form of reproving the wrongdoer. When a parent punishes a child, she is not repaying evil with evil; she is reproving the child. When reproval is done properly, it is an example of "overcoming evil with good." Paul was probably acquainted with the passage in Leviticus 19:17–18 that reads:

You shall not hate in your heart anyone of your kin; you shall reprove your neighbor, or you will incur guilt yourself. You shall not take vengeance or bear a grudge against any of your people, but you shall love your neighbor as yourself.

Reproving your neighbor, when done in the right way, is an example of loving your neighbor.

The tension that interpreters have thought they saw between chapters 12 and 13 is not there. God does not assign government to do what he forbids individual believers to do, namely, exercise vengeance or retribution.

Let us now look more closely at what Paul says about the task of the state. Calvin, along with most other traditional commentators, takes the last clause of verse 1 as the center of his interpretation: "those authorities that exist have been instituted by God." He interprets this as meaning two things: whoever may be the head of government over a certain populace, God has brought it about that he or she is the head; and to be the head of government over a certain populace is to be in a position of authority over it. The concept of authority that Calvin employs in his interpretation of verse 1 is the concept that I called, in the preceding chapter, *positional authority.*

Calvin then interprets verse 4 as telling us what those in positions of governmental authority ought to do. They ought to execute wrath on wrongdoers, broadly understood. Often they don't do that; they fail to punish wrongdoers and they tyrannize those who do good. But as we have seen, it was Calvin's view that their failure to act as they morally ought to act does not undermine their positional authority, provided that they act within the scope of their jurisdiction; on this he was right.

I submit that the center of interpretation should not be verse 1 but verses 4 and 5. Government is a servant of God. As a servant of God, it has a God-assigned task to perform. Its God-assigned task is to exercise governance over the public for the purpose of executing wrath or anger on wrongdoers, thereby indicating its support of doing good. If God assigns it that task, then God both authorizes and enjoins it to perform that task. And if God authorizes it to perform that task, then it has the authority to do that, the God-given authority to exercise governance over the public for the purpose of executing wrath on wrongdoers and thereby indicating its support of doing good. The concept of authority that Paul is employing is not the concept of being in an institutional position of authority but the concept of having the authority to do something.[4]

As to what God authorizes the state to do, I am reminded of a way of understanding punishment that has recently entered the lists and that I find compelling, the so-called *expressive* theory. (I hinted at this way of understanding punishment a few paragraphs back.) The expressive theory says that punishment of a wrongdoer should not be understood as retribution – redressing

---

[4] In my essay "'For the Authorities are God's Servants': Is a Theistic Account of Political Authority Still Viable or Have Humanist Accounts Won the Day?" I distinguish between someone with authority *deputizing* someone to exercise authority on his behalf and someone with authority *delegating* some of his authority to someone; and I argue that Paul's account of the authority of the state vis-à-vis God is implicitly a delegation account, not a deputy account. Here in this discussion I speak of God *commissioning and authorizing* the state; the idea is the same as *delegating*. The essay can be found in Ken Grasso and Cecilia Castillo, eds., *Theology and Public Philosophy* (Lanham, MD: Rowman & Littlefield, forthcoming).

harm with harm – but as a way of reproving what he did and of expressing anger at him for having done it. Speaking anachronistically, Paul was employing the expressive theory of punishment rather than the retributive theory in stating what God assigns government to do.[5]

Whose anger do governmental authorities execute on wrongdoers? Paul doesn't say. He just says that God has appointed governments to serve God by executing anger on wrongdoers. In particular, he does not say that it is *God's* anger that governments are appointed to execute.[6] Paul leaves no doubt in Romans that God is angry at wrongdoing. But he does not say that God *deputizes* governments to execute anger *on God's behalf.* Nowhere in the passage do we find the language of deputy, vicegerent, proxy, and the like, not even a hint of Calvin's divine-deputy account of governmental authority. One can appoint someone to be one's servant for accomplishing some task without making them one's deputy, one's proxy. Paul does not say that the state's issuing some directive counts as God's issuing that directive.

I think we can infer, from the social benefits that Paul cites of government carrying out its assignment, that we would interpret him in too pinched and literalistic a fashion if we held that it was *only* punishment, strictly speaking, that he had in mind. The two main benefits Paul cites are being a deterrent to bad conduct and signaling support for good conduct. Paul's thought, so I suggest, is that God has assigned government the task not just of *punishing*

---

[5] I explain and defend the expressive theory at some length in chapter 17 of my *Justice in Love*.
[6] The Revised Standard Version translates the last clause of 13:4 thus: "he is the servant of God to execute his wrath on the wrongdoer." But "his," referring back to God, is an interpretive interpolation on the part of the Revised Standard Version translators.

wrongdoing once it has occurred, but also of *deterring* its occurrence and of *protecting* the public from its occurrence.

Government does this by publishing a law code which specifies actions that are forbidden and which attaches coercive sanctions to those laws, by establishing a judiciary to determine whether someone has violated the law and to order a punishment in case it determines that he has, by setting up a police force to prevent or deter violations of the law, and by maintaining a military. It's this whole fourfold system that brings about the social benefits Paul cites of executing anger on wrongdoers, namely, making those who are contemplating doing wrong fearful of doing so and signaling support for doing good. So let us henceforth understand Paul's words "execute anger on the wrongdoer" as a synecdoche for that more comprehensive task. The God-assigned task of government is to exercise governance over the public for the purpose of *curbing wrongdoing*.

Government cannot curb all wrongdoing; it lacks the resources. To insult someone is to wrong her; but no government has the resources to curb all insults. Government has to set priorities, overlooking minor forms of wrongdoing and focusing on the serious.

To wrong someone is to deprive her of something to which she has a right, a legitimate claim. And to deprive her of something to which she has a right or a legitimate claim is to treat her unjustly. So instead of saying that it is the God-assigned task of government to curb wrongdoing, we could say that it is the God-assigned task of government to *curb injustice*. Or we could say that it is the God-assigned task of government *to protect the rights* of the public. God has assigned government the task of being a *rights-protecting* institution. Three different ways of expressing the same idea.

What types of injustice has God assigned government to curb? Paul doesn't say. He knows nothing of our distinction between economic injustice and political injustice, nothing of our distinction between economic rights and political rights. If he had known of the distinction, he would surely have regarded it as irrelevant. What he would have learned from his study of "the law and the prophets" was that the king, when carrying out his assignment to establish justice in the land, was to give priority to the downtrodden: the widows, the orphans, the aliens, and the impoverished. These are the ones for whom injustice is not an occasional assault but a daily condition; that's why they have priority. If there are people in society who are deprived of fair access to medical care or to adequate means of sustenance, then it is the God-assigned task of government to undo this injustice. Exactly how government can best undo some injustice depends on circumstances; different means fit different situations. But government does not have the option of ignoring the unjust condition of those at the bottom of the ladder of social power.

Because God has authorized and enjoined government to exercise governance over the public for the purpose of curbing injustice, the people must submit, says Paul; they must obey, be subject, conform (the verb is *hypotassō*). Paul does not say that they are to submit because government officials are "in a position of authority" or because they "have authority." Neither here nor elsewhere does he employ the concept of positional authority. He says they are to submit because God has appointed government to serve God by curbing injustice. For the same reason they are to render to the governmental authorities what is due them: taxes to those who are due taxes, respect to those who are due respect, honor to those who are due honor.

The injunction to submit leaves open the question of the reason for submitting. Paul answers that question when he says that they are to submit "not only out of wrath but also because of conscience [*syneidêsin*]." By "out of wrath" Paul surely means, out of fear of sanctions. Paul does not condemn submitting because one judges that one is likely to be punished if one does not submit; what he emphasizes, however, is that the people are to submit out of conscience. Along with most commentators I interpret this as meaning that they are *morally obligated to submit*. The directives that the government issues to the public for the purpose of curbing injustice are binding.

But suppose government itself becomes a wrongdoer. This can take at least four forms. Government might turn a blind eye to serious wrongdoing among the citizens and those living or traveling within its territory. It might issue directives to citizens and others that amount to commanding them to do wrong. It might itself directly wrong citizens and others by the directives it issues to them, denying them their right to religious freedom, their right to assemble, and so forth. Or it might itself directly wrong citizens and foreigners by the sort of force and coercion it applies to them.

If God commissions government to exercise governance over the public for the purpose of executing wrath on wrongdoers, then obviously God does not authorize government itself to become a wrongdoer in any of these ways. All such actions fall outside the divine authorization. We can say something stronger. Not only does God's authorization not extend to authorizing the state itself to become a wrongdoer; God does not *permit* the government to issue directives or employ forms of coercion that constitute wrongdoing on the part of the government. What sense would it make for God to commission government to exercise governance over the public for the purpose of executing anger against individual wrongdoers while permitting government itself to be a wrongdoer?

God's commissioning – authorizing and enjoining – the state to exercise governance over the public for the purpose of executing wrath on wrongdoers thus implies that the state is to be a *rights-honoring* state, or if one prefers, a *rights-limited* state. The authority of the state is limited by the rights of the members of the public. Earlier I observed that no government has the resources to curb all wrongdoing; it has to set priorities and overlook minor wrongs. What must be added is that even if the government does have the resources to curb a certain form of wrongdoing, it must refrain if doing so would require a more serious wronging of the public than the wronging it was trying to curb.

Paul neither says nor suggests that if officials in a position of authority order the members of the public to do something and that order falls within the scope of their positional authority, then it generates in the public the obligation to obey. The reason he neither says nor suggests this is that he is not working with the concept of positional authority but with the concept of performance-authority, or, more specifically, with the concept of authority to govern. God commissions government to do something, namely, to exercise governance over the public with the aim of curbing injustice. And as we saw in Chapter 6, if the state is not morally permitted to issue a certain directive to the public, then, if it nonetheless does so, its doing so does not generate in the public the obligation to obey. The directive is not binding. The fact that it was issued by officials in a position of authority and that it falls within the scope of their positional authority makes no difference.

It's time to turn to the two opening verses of Romans 13; as I mentioned earlier, it was Calvin's interpretation of these verses that governed his interpretation of the passage as a whole and decisively shaped his views on political authority and political obedience.

I suggest that Paul is saying substantially the same thing in these first two verses that he says, with amplification, in verses 4 and 5; it's because of the amplification that we should take 4 and 5 as the center of our interpretation and interpret verses 1 and 2 in their light rather than the other way around.

"Let every person be subject to the governing authorities," says Paul. The verb translated here as "subject" is the same as the one translated as "subject" in verse 5, namely, *hypotassô*.

Why should everybody be subject to the governing authorities? Because "those authorities that exist have been instituted by God." With verse 4 in mind, our immediate thought is that they are not just instituted, *period, full stop*. That's how the passage has traditionally been read, with interpreters tossing off suggestions as to what Paul might mean by saying that God "institutes" governing authorities. From verse 4 we know that they are instituted *to do* something, appointed to *do* something; and we know what that is, namely, to curb injustice.

When the sentence is understood as elliptical in this way, "instituted" proves a rather poor translation of the verb *tassô*; better is the first meaning that my Greek–English lexicon gives for the verb, namely, "appointed." They are *appointed*, appointed *to do* something; "appointed" is the translation that the New Revised Standard Version gives for the word *diatagê* in verse 2. Governing authorities are appointed by God to exercise governance over the public for the purpose of executing anger on wrongdoers, in that way to serve God. They are commissioned by God to do this, assigned to do this, thereby authorized and enjoined to do this. And so it is that when they do what they are assigned to do, we must not resist them but obey and submit; to resist them would be to resist what God has assigned them to do, authorized and enjoined them to do. This is how the argument will be fleshed out in verses 4 and 5. In verses 1 and 2 the full argument is alluded to but not fleshed out.

Calvin, along with countless other commentators, interpreted Paul's declaration that "those authorities that exist have been instituted by God" as the declaration that whoever is in a position of governmental authority has been placed in that position by God. But if we agree that verses 4 and 5 flesh out Paul's thought in the two opening verses, then that is an exceedingly implausible interpretation – completely *ad hoc*, unrelated to the main argument. Paul is not saying that whoever occupies some position of governmental authority does so because God has put him in that position; he is saying that whoever finds himself in such a position, however that came about, has a commission from God, an assignment, to serve God by exercising governance over the public for the purpose of executing anger on wrongdoers.

Last, what about that other clause in verse 1, "there is no authority except from God"? I think it highly unlikely that Paul is here inserting into his argument an abstract comment about authority in general; possible, but unlikely. He's talking about the authority of what he calls "governing authorities." I also think it highly unlikely that he is answering your and my question as to whether it is possible to account for political authority from below, or whether only an account from above can work. Many centuries will elapse before that question gets asked. What Paul is saying is that resisting the government, when the government is carrying out its God-assigned task, is never merely resisting the government but always resisting something else as well. That something else is God – not some Roman deity, not one of those transcendent authorities or powers of which Paul speaks in other places.

Governmental authorities have been assigned by God to deter, prevent, and punish wrongdoing. No heavenly being other than God has assigned them to do this.

One issue of interpretation remains. What was Paul saying, about God and God's justice, when in 12:19 he said, "Beloved, never avenge yourselves, but leave room for the wrath of God; for it is written, 'Vengeance is mine, I will repay, says the Lord'"? The passage plays a role in Paul's injunction to individual believers as to how they are to conduct themselves; it plays no role in the account of the task of the state that Paul gives in chapter 13. Since our topic here is Paul's teaching concerning the task of the state, nothing would be lost if we simply moved on. But the passage cries out for an interpretation.

The Letter to the Romans as a whole, or at least the first thirteen chapters thereof, is an extended discussion of certain aspects of how God deals with human wrongdoing, the assumption throughout being that God is by no means indifferent to human wrongdoing. Quite the contrary: God is angry at human wrongdoing (1:18). What Paul then says in 12:19 is that believers are to conduct themselves in such a way as to leave room for the anger of God at human wrongdoing; they are not to "play God."

That much is clear. What is not clear is the thought behind Paul's next statement, quoting Deuteronomy 32:35, that "'Vengeance is mine, I will repay, says the Lord.'"

The aspect of God's way of dealing with human wrongdoing to which Paul devotes the bulk of his attention in Romans is God's offer of justification to all who have faith in God. The overall theme of the book is that God shows no partiality in his offer of justification; God offers justification to Jews and Gentiles alike. God's offer of justification is just, fair, equitable. The other aspect of God's way of dealing with human wrongdoing to which Paul devotes his attention in Romans is the aspect that we have been discussing in this chapter: God authorizes and enjoins the state to curb human wrongdoing.

There are other aspects of God's way of dealing with human wrongdoing that lie in the background of Paul's discussion in Romans but are not brought to the fore as a topic of discussion. One of these background aspects is God's forbearance of human wrongdoing. In 3:25 Paul says that in "divine forbearance [God] had passed over former sins" (see also 2:4 and 9:22). The effect of God's forbearing human wrongdoing, of putting up with it, is that God "gives up" wrongdoers to "the lusts of their hearts to impurity" (1:24), to "dishonorable passions" (1:26), "to a base mind and to improper conduct" (1:28). You and I could cite many other effects of God's toleration of human wrongdoing.

It was of the Gentiles that Paul was speaking when he spoke of forbearance. In her book *Paul Was Not a Christian: The Original Message of a Misunderstood Apostle*, Paula Eisenbaum argues that Paul was expressing the same tradition as that expressed by 2 Maccabees:

> For in the case of the other nations the Lord waits patiently to punish them until they have reached the full measure of their sins; but he does not deal in this way with us, in order that he should not take vengeance on us afterward when our sins have reached their height. Therefore he never withdraws his mercy from us. Although he disciplines us with calamities, he does not forsake his own people. (2 Maccabees 6:14–16)[7]

God does not forbear Israel's wrongdoing; God does not put up with it. But neither does God take vengeance on Israel. Instead God disciplines Israel, reproves her. God's treatment of Israel is like a parent's punishment of her child.

---

[7] Paula Eisenbaum, *Paul Was Not a Christian: The Original Message of a Misunderstood Apostle* (New York: HarperOne, 2009), pp. 220–21.

Though God forbears the wrongdoing of the other nations, forbearance is not the last word. Eventually God judges and punishes the nations. What Romans 12:19 says is that God's punishment of the other nations takes the form of retribution. Paul does not explain how God's retributive punishment of the nations fits together with God's offer of justification to all members of all nations – though what can be said, of course, is that God does not "take vengeance" on anyone who accepts God's offer of justification.

It's not our business to deal with the mass of human wrongdoing; that's God's business. God's way of dealing with the mass of human wrongdoing will have a dimension of retribution. Believers are not to imitate God in that respect. They are not to avenge themselves. They are not to repay evil with evil, harm with harm. They are instead to return evil with good. If one's enemy is hungry, feed him; if he is thirsty, give him something to drink.

Paul's teaching in Romans 13 leaves you and me with many questions. Do states have the authority to exercise governance over the public for purposes other than curbing injustice – to coordinate certain actions of the citizens, for example, to provide infrastructure of various sorts, to provide benefits of certain kinds even when it cannot be argued that justice requires it? Nothing Paul says implies that states do not have such authority; I myself think it highly unlikely that he thought the Roman Empire had exceeded its authority when it built its network of roads. All we can say is that he does not cite such authority as bestowed on the state by God.

It would be a serious mistake, however, to allow this and other silences on Paul's part to obscure from view the significance of what he is not silent about, the significance of what he has said. The God-given task of government is not to pressure citizens into becoming virtuous and pious; its God-given task is instead to pressure citizens into not perpetrating injustice. Though it is not inconsistent with what Paul says to hold that government has the authority to seek various social goods, we should not fail to be struck by the fact that what he cites as the God-given task of government is deterring, punishing, and protecting against wrongdoing. God authorizes and enjoins the state to be a rights-protecting institution. This implies, as we saw, that it is also to be a rights-limited or rights-honoring institution.

I mentioned at the beginning of this chapter that the novelty of the situation Paul was addressing – how the members of the church are to relate to the Roman Empire – did not lead him to offer a substantially new answer to the question of political authority and obedience. The picture of political authority and obedience that he offered to the Roman Christians was essentially the same as that which dominates the Old Testament, or Hebrew Bible. The central task of the ruler is to secure justice. In Psalm 72 we get a classic presentation:

> Give the king thy justice, O God,
>   and thy righteousness to the royal son!
> May he judge thy people with righteousness,
>   and thy poor with justice!
> Let the mountains bear prosperity for the people,
>   and the hills, in righteousness!
> May he defend the cause of the poor of the people,
>   give deliverance to the needy,
>   and crush the oppressor.[8]

---

[8] In this essay I do not address the question of whether all the biblical passages that speak to the relation between divine and political authority can be interpreted in harmony with Paul's teaching in Romans 13, or whether there are some that contradict his teaching. To the best of my knowledge there is none that contradicts Paul's teaching. But here my project is not to look at the totality of what Christian scripture says on this topic but to follow the tradition in taking Paul's teaching in Romans 13 as the *locus classicus*.

Compare and contrast this picture of the ruler, and Paul's adaptation of it, with that found in the opening pages of Aristotle's *Politics*. Here is how Aristotle begins his discussion:

Every state is a community of some kind, and every community is established with a view to some good; for everyone always acts in order to obtain that which they think good. But, if all communities aim at some good, the state or political community, which is the highest of all, and which embraces all the rest, aims at good in a greater degree than any other, and at the highest good. (*Politics*, 1252^a 1–6)[9]

After discussing the dynamics in human nature that lead to the formation of such small-scale communities as families and villages, Aristotle then goes on to say this:

When several villages are united in a single complete community, large enough to be nearly or quite self-sufficing, the state comes into existence, originating in the bare needs of life, and continuing in existence for the sake of a good life. And therefore, if the earlier forms of society are natural, so is the state, for it is the end of them and the nature of a thing is its end.

Hence it is evident that the state is a creation of nature, and that man is by nature a political animal. (Ibid., 1252^b 28–1253^a 3)

Aristotle claims that there is a dynamic in human nature that leads to the formation of larger and larger communities until we arrive at political communities and at the states that govern those communities; Paul teaches that God commissions the state to perform a certain task. There is no contradiction here. Paul neither says nor implies that there is no such dynamic in human beings as that to which Aristotle points. Whatever it is in human nature that leads to the formation of states, God authorizes and enjoins the states that come into being to secure justice.

---

[9] I am using the translation in *The Complete Works of Aristotle*, ed. Jonathan Barnes (Princeton University Press, 1984).

Paul would, however, dispute Aristotle's claim that the state or political community is the highest of all, that it embraces all the others, and that it aims at good to a higher degree than any other institution and aims at the highest good. As we shall see in Chapter 11, the existence and nature of the church make it impossible for Paul to accept that picture of the state. The church is not embraced by the state; and the good it aims at is higher than the good the state aims at.

But this point, concerning the political implications of the nature and existence of the church, is only implicit in Romans 13. The obvious point of disagreement between what Aristotle says in the passages quoted and what Paul says in Romans 13 is over what Aristotle cites as the *telos* of the state. Aristotle declares that the state has some social good as its *telos*. In these passages he does not say what that is; later in the *Politics* (and in the *Nichomachean Ethics*) we learn that the social good at which the state aims includes cultivating virtue in the citizenry – making the citizens good. Addressing the Roman Christians, Paul makes the similar-sounding declaration that government's doing what it is assigned to do is "for your good." But the good he has in mind is not that of virtue in the citizenry but the good of curbing wrongdoing and encouraging the good-doing that such curbing naturally brings in its wake As to our becoming good human beings, "well-pleasing" to God, Paul would say that for that we must look elsewhere than to the state.

These are two very different ways of thinking about the task of the state. One says that the task of the state is to promote virtue in the citizens. The other says that the God-given task of the state is to protect citizens from being wronged, this having the effect of encouraging a certain minimal virtue in the citizens. The former view is often called a *perfectionist* view of the task of the state; the latter might be called a *protectionist* view The latter way of thinking implies limits on what the state may do; the rights-protecting state must be a rights-honoring state. The former way of thinking does not imply limits. If achieving some social good requires imposing misery on some of the public, one does not ask whether imposing that misery constitutes violating the rights of those citizens; one asks whether the good of the end outweighs the evil of the misery.

To conclude this chapter, let's return to an issue raised at the beginning of the preceding chapter: would the success of one or another account from below of political authority render irrelevant an account of political authority from above? I said that the question should be answered with a No; I added, however, that I would say no more on the matter until we had in hand an account of the relation between divine authority and political authority.

I hold that it is in fact possible to give an account of political authority from below; in my essay "Accounting for the Political Authority of the State," I offer such an account.[10] The core of the account I offer is that we each have a natural right to there being, when possible, some institutionalized arrangement for protecting us against being seriously wronged by our fellows. In the modern world, that institutionalized arrangement is the state. We each have a right to the state exercising governance over the public for the purpose of protecting us against being ser-iously wronged by our fellows; and the state has the correlative duty to exercise governance over the public for the purpose of protecting members of the public from being wronged by their

[10] The essay is included in my *Understanding Liberal Democracy*, ed. Terence Cuneo (Oxford University Press, forthcoming).

fellows. The state does this by establishing a system of laws, enforcing those laws, adjudicating alleged breaches of the laws, and maintaining a military. If the state has the duty to do this, then it has the authority to do this. The reader will notice the close similarity between what the state has the authority to do, on this account from below, and what the state is authorized to do on Paul's account from above.

We sometimes promise to do what we were already obligated to do. When we do that, we have two reasons for doing the thing in question: we were already obligated to do it, and now our promise has generated in us the obligation to keep our promise by doing the thing promised. So too we sometimes command or request that someone do something that they were already obligated to do. The recipient of the command then has two reasons for doing the thing commanded: he was already obligated to do it, and now our command has generated in him the obligation to obey by doing the thing commanded. And sometimes we authorize someone to do something that he already had the authority to do.

Why do we do these things? Why don't we limit our promises to things we were not previously obligated to do? Why don't we limit our commands to things the addressee was not previously obligated to do? Why don't we limit our authorizations to things the recipients were not previously authorized to do?

The reason why we don't limit ourselves in these ways is that promising, commanding, and authorizing introduce a new and important interpersonal factor into the situation. Now, after promising you to do something, I let you down if I don't do it; I break my commitment to you. That was not true before. Now, after commanding you to do something that I have the *potestas* and the right to command you to do, you slight me if you do not do that.

That was not true before. The state may already have had political authority from below to curb wrongdoing. God's authorizing and enjoining it to curb wrongdoing means that its failure to do so is defiance of God. That was not true before.[11]

---

[11] Kevin Vallier has pressed me on whether my claim that it is possible to give an account from below of the political authority of the state is compatible with Christian scripture. He cites Matthew 18:18, where Jesus says, "All authority on heaven and earth has been given to me." I think it extremely unlikely that Jesus is here speaking either about authority to govern in general, or about that specific version of authority to govern that the state possesses. He is authorizing his disciples to depart from Israel and disciple the nations. Immediately after the sentence quoted he says, "Go therefore and make disciples of all nations." Kevin also cites John 19:11 in the English Standard Version translation. Jesus is speaking to Pilate. "You would have no authority over me at all unless it had been given you from above." The New Revised Standard Version translates the Greek term *exousia* here as "power." I think that this translation is likely correct. Pilate has just said, "do you not know that I have power [*exousia*] to release you, and power [*exousia*] to crucify you?" Quite clearly it is his power that Pilate is here referring to; if that is correct, then Jesus' reply also refers not to authority but to power.

CHAPTER 9

God's governance of humankind

We saw in the preceding chapter that God's governance of humankind takes the form of God authorizing and enjoining the state to exercise governance over the public so as to curb wrongdoing. But this is by no means the only form taken by God's governance of humankind. If the state is to curb wrongdoing, we human beings must be able to discern what constitutes wrongdoing. In our capacity to tell right from wrong, Paul discerns God's *moral* governance of humankind (Romans 1). God's political governance presupposes God's moral governance. So let us take a step back and look at God's moral governance of humankind. The topic deserves a book; here I will give it only a few pages. That done, let us then consider how God's authorization of government to curb wrongdoing fits within this larger picture.

Unlike other animals, we human beings are not such that our nature determines what we do; we are free agents, capable of acting for reasons and not only out of causes. But God did not create us as free agents and then set us loose to act as we see fit. God exercises governance over humankind by issuing directives to us for how we are to treat God, how we are to treat each other and ourselves, and how we are to treat nature. All directives concerning God and each other are specifications of two fundamental directives: we are to love God with our whole being and to love our neighbors as ourselves. The directive to love one's neighbor as oneself incorporates the injunction to treat the neighbor justly.[1] We are to *care about* the neighbor as we do about ourselves.

Jesus declared these two directives to be the greatest in the Torah, its sum and substance; his interlocutors agreed. Torah was of course issued to Israel. But the two fundamental love-directives have been issued to all humankind, not just to Israel; it's only their issuance in the form of Torah that was unique to Israel. We are all to love God and to care about the neighbor as we do about ourselves; we owe it to God to do so.

We should not take it as obvious that God's governance of humankind would take the form of God's directing us to love God and neighbor. Most of the gods that human beings have imagined either have had no interest in exercising governance over human beings or have been interested in exercising governance over only some of us. And as for those gods who were interested in exercising governance over human beings in general, their governance was not to the end that we would love God with our whole being and our neighbors as ourselves. It was to the end that we would fear and placate the gods, or treat our rulers as divine, or enslave foreigners, or seek revenge on those who wrong us, and so forth.

Let me quote a passage on this topic from the Israeli scholar of antiquity Yochanan Muffs. After remarking that the "very center" of biblical prophecy is "divine concern with man," he says:

One should not take this display of interest too lightly, for the true turning of God toward man was a total revolution in the religious world of the ancient Near East. The gods of Babylonia were completely dependent on nature and fate. Their major interest was themselves: the satisfaction of their needs, their hates, and their loves. The gods of

---

[1] I defend this claim at length in my *Justice in Love* (Grand Rapids: Wm. B. Eerdmans Publishing Co., 2011).

Babylonia were not interested in the private destiny of man. To satisfy their physical needs, they turned only to the king.[2]

Even when the pagan gods take an interest in the lives of individual kings, the demands imposed on the latter are essentially cultic ... The essential demand of the God of Israel, on the other hand, is not cultic. Rather, the biblical God demands moral behavior from His people.[3]

The issuing of directives to human beings for how they are to comport themselves is necessary but not sufficient for governance to take place; the recipients must know those directives and follow them, conform to them. Otherwise the one who issues the directives says, "I haven't succeeded in governing them." So the question we must ask is, how is God's moral governance of humankind effectuated, actualized, realized? One imagines that it might have been actualized by God bringing it about that each and every one of us had the vivid sense of being in the presence of God and of God speaking to us and telling us that we are to love God and neighbor – and of our then obeying out of awe for the staggering majesty of the one who commanded us. Obviously that's not how it works.

In part, God effectuates God's governance over how we treat each other by way of two factors in human nature. One is the factor that the eighteenth-century Scots moral theorists called the sentiment of benevolence, which I prefer to call *the impulse toward caring about the other*. This impulse enlists other dynamics within human nature in its support: the dynamic of attachment to the other, the dynamic of identification with the other, the dynamic of sympathy or empathy for the plight of the other, the dynamic of compassion or pity, and so on; but its effects are wider than any

---

[2] Yochanan Muffs, *The Personhood of God: Biblical Theology, Human Faith and the Divine Image* (Woodstock, VT: Jewish Lights Publishing Co., 2005), p. 14.
[3] Ibid., p. 26.

of those. And while it is often supported by those other dynamics, it is also easily and commonly blocked and inhibited. To use scriptural language, the heart is often hardened – hardened by stories we tell about the other, hardened by categories we employ to describe the other, hardened by apprehension at the prospect of what it would cost us if we softened our heart to the other. Yet the existence of the impulse cannot be denied. I write these words one week after the January 2010 earthquake in Haiti. What else would account for the outpouring of aid? The human being in whom there is no "milk of human kindness" is a malformed human being; there's something wrong with him or her.

The second factor is our capacity for discerning our duties toward the other and her rights against us, and our disposition toward acting on that discernment by doing our duties and honoring her rights. Call this our *capacity and disposition for moral action.* Obviously our capacity and disposition for moral action is as readily and frequently inhibited as our impulse toward caring about the other – perhaps even more readily and frequently inhibited. We do what we ought not to do and do not do what we ought to do. Nonetheless the existence of this capacity can also not be denied. The psychopath (sociopath) talks a good moral line, but his talk doesn't gear into what he does. Such a person is malformed; there's something wrong with him.

There has been a flurry of discussion in recent years concerning the origin of these two factors in human beings. Are they innate or are they the result of learning of some sort? If they are learned, just how does the learning take place? If they are innate, is there a module in the brain for one or both of them? What role is played by emotions in the workings of these two factors? Is there some plausible evolutionary story to tell about how it came about that these factors are part of our nature? Interesting as some of these discussions are, it would distract from our purposes here to enter them.

One comment should be made, however. The impression one gets from some of these discussions is that these two factors work more or less automatically, without any significant intervention of reason. Surely that's mistaken. Some of their workings are more or less automatic; that's how it has to be. But we also learn about our rights and duties by thinking about them, thinking about them as the occasion demands but also thinking about them in the sustained, systematic, and non-occasional manner of the long tradition of normative ethics – or as it used to be called, "casuistry." And sometimes our hard heart toward certain human beings is softened by learning from scholars that the stories we told each other are false.

The factors in human nature that I have identified yield the result that Paul points to in Romans 1:14–15 when he speaks of Gentiles who "do by nature" what the law requires. What the law requires is "written on their hearts"; their "conscience bears witness" to it. They are, as it were, "a law to themselves"; that is, it's not by way of something outside themselves but by virtue of their nature that they know the moral law.

Jews and Christians hold that there is another way as well in which God exercises moral governance over humankind. I alluded to this other way earlier. It consists of God speaking to human beings by way of the law and the prophets of Israel and by way of Jesus of Nazareth. This is not human nature at work; this is God speaking by way of human beings speaking.[4] The content of this speech of God has now spread throughout all nations.

---

[4] Muslims hold a comparable view, of course, for God's speech to Mohammed.

God's moral governance of human beings is the context for Paul's teaching in Romans 13 concerning what it is that God authorizes government to do. I have called attention to the fact that the two fundamental factors in human nature that account for the effectuating of God's moral governance, the impulse toward caring about the other and the capacity and disposition for moral discernment and action, are all too easily and all too commonly subject to inhibition and malformation. Rational reflection and listening to God's speech go a long way toward dealing with our ignorance, willful and non-willful, as to what justice requires and what serves the good of the neighbor. But they do not deal with our resistance. In Romans 13 Paul presents government as playing the role, in the effectuating of God's governance, of serving as the main enforcement mechanism in society. God authorizes and enjoins government to serve this function, not to coerce us into loving God and neighbor, if that were even possible, but to deter and punish our wronging of the other and thereby, at the same time, to encourage our doing of what is good and right.

Government is not and could not be the totality of the means that God employs for governance of humankind. It's only one component in the effectuation of the governance; I called it "the enforcement mechanism." The enforcement mechanism does its work within the broader context of God's multifaceted governance of humankind.

CHAPTER 10

Recap

Before we move on to discuss the duality of Christians being members of the church and also citizens of the state, hence under dual authority, let us take stock of the conclusions we have reached concerning the relation between God's authority and the political authority of the state.

I have taken for granted that God has authority over human beings, in particular, the authority to exercise governance over us and the authority to authorize the state to exercise political governance over its citizens. That God does have such authority is the dominant position in the Christian tradition, as it is in the Jewish and Islamic traditions. I have gone along with the tradition on this point. Someone who does not go along with that tradition, either because they think God does not exist or because they think God does not have authority over human beings, will regard our project in this essay as misguided from the ground up.

A full treatment of our topic would include an account of God's authority; among other things, such an account would identify the ground of God's authority and would analyze the various modes of divine authority. Though such an account would be relevant and desirable, it's not necessary for our project in this essay. Nor have I presupposed such an account. Following Paul, I have done no more than claim that God has authorized the state to be his servant in curbing wrongdoing and securing justice. That claim is not an implication of some account or theory of divine authority that I have tacitly embraced; it's a datum that any Christian account of divine authority must comport with and illuminate.

Contrary to what the term suggests, political theology is not theology. It is not discourse about God with a political cast. That's what a freestanding account of the nature and grounds of God's authority would be: discourse about God with a political cast. The subject of political theology is not God but the state. It is not a branch of theology but a species of political theory, namely, *theological* political theory. Theology is the modifier, political theory the substantive. The task of political theology is to develop a theological account of the state and of its relation to various other realities. In this essay I focus exclusively on the relation of the authority of the state to God's authority and on the relation of the authority of the state to the authority of the church.

A full treatment of our topic would also include a theoretical elaboration of the moral epistemology to which I appealed in the preceding chapter. Though such a theory would be relevant and desirable, it too is not necessary for our project. Nor have I tacitly presupposed any theory of moral epistemology. What I presented was, in my judgment, no more than data that any such theory has to be compatible with and illuminate.

I placed Paul's teaching in Romans 13 at the center of my reflections on the authority of the state and on the relation of that authority to God's authority. Romans 13 has always been central in the long tradition of Christian political theology. If I had been content simply to add to that tradition, I could have left Paul in the shadows, on the ground that the tradition has long ago absorbed what he had to say. But I came to the conclusion that the main tradition has misinterpreted Paul's text and that, as a consequence, it has taken a wrong turn at several points. Showing where it has taken a wrong turn and pointing to the path ahead required grappling with Paul's text. My reflections on the relation between God's authority and the political authority of the state have thus been, in effect, Pauline reflections.

What Paul says concerning the relation between God's authority and the political authority of the state presupposes that God loves justice or, more precisely, that God desires that justice be done in a world where we human beings often treat each other unjustly. It presupposes that God desires that injustice be curbed. To this end, God commissions or appoints the state to function as his servant for punishing, deterring, and protecting against wrongdoing. God's commissioning the state to do those things amounts to God's authorizing and enjoining it to do them – authorizing and enjoining it to exercise governance over the public for the purpose of maintaining a system for curbing injustice. Given the connection between justice and rights, we can say that God authorizes and enjoins the state to be the supreme rights-protecting institution in society. This implies, as we saw, that the state must not itself become a wrongdoer. In its actions it is to be rights-honoring, and thereby rights-limited.

The corollary to God's authorizing the state to exercise governance over the public for the purpose of curbing injustice is that the public is obligated to obey such directives as the state may issue in the course of carrying out its God-given assignment. When the state acts for the purpose of curbing injustice in society, its directives are binding; they generate in the public the obligation to obey. Hence it is that Paul couples his declaration that God has commissioned the state to be his servant, by establishing a system for curbing injustice, with injunctions to his readers to obey the government, and beyond that to honor it.

And what if the state goes beyond seeking to curb injustice and aims to enhance the common good – builds infrastructure that is of benefit to everybody, coordinates the activities of citizens, develops public parks, and builds public museums? Does the state have the authority to do such things or is it exceeding its authority?

Nothing Paul says suggests an answer one way or the other. From the fact that God authorized the state to curb injustice it does not follow that the state lacks authority to enhance the common good in ways that go beyond what justice requires. The state might have authority from below for that. Or it might have authority from above – by virtue of God commissioning it to do something else than what Paul mentions in Romans.

God's desire that injustice be curbed is by no means the full extent of God's desire for humankind. God desires shalom, the flourishing of the people. Shalom goes beyond the absence of injustice. In the modern world, states serve this desire of God for shalom by doing the sorts of things mentioned above: building infrastructure, securing coordination of activities, founding and maintaining institutions and landscapes that are of public benefit. Perhaps, starting from God's desire for shalom, one could develop an argument for the conclusion that God has authorized government to do such things, provided that its doing them does not come at the cost of wronging individuals, institutions, or the people as a whole.

But suppose that my government, rather than going beyond what justice requires, acts in violation of what justice requires. It directs me to wrong one of my fellows, or it deprives me of that to which I have a right and directs me to submit to the deprivation without resistance or protest.

In such a case, there can be no doubt concerning divine authorization. God never has authorized and never will authorize the government to issue such directives. And if the government has no divine authorization to issue such directives, then obviously

I have no obligation to obey such directives on account of the government's having been authorized by God to issue them.[1]

We saw that something stronger and more general can be said. A condition of some directive generating in me the moral obligation to obey is that it be morally permissible for the entity which issued the directive to do so. But it's not morally permissible for the government to direct me to wrong one of my fellows, nor is it morally permissible for the government to direct me to submit without resistance or protest to its wronging of me.

It is on this last point that the theological account of political authority and obligation that I have derived and extrapolated from Paul's discussion in Romans differs most sharply from traditional accounts. The concept of authority that I have interpreted Paul as employing in Romans is the concept of what I have called *performance-authority*, the authority to do something. God commissions governments to do something, namely, to serve God by curbing injustice, thereby giving support to those who act justly.

Traditionally it was assumed that Paul was instead employing the concept of *positional authority* – the authority to issue directives by virtue of legitimately occupying some institutional position of authority. Given this assumption, Paul was then interpreted as teaching that whoever legitimately occupies some position of authority in the government has been placed in that position by God. And this was thought to imply that if some government official has the positional authority to issue a certain directive – doing so falls within the scope of what his office authorizes him to do – then God authorizes him to issue that directive and we, correspondingly, are obligated to obey. Calvin went so far as to say that the official is

---

[1] The obligation here is what is sometimes called *objective* obligation. If I believe, and am entitled to believe, about some such directive that God has authorized the government to issue it, then I am *subjectively* obligated to obey. I am blamable if I do not.

God's deputy or proxy: some government official directing me to do something *counts as* God directing me to do that.

It's obvious that government officials issue many directives that morally they ought not to issue but that their office nonetheless entitles them to issue; they have positional authority to issue those directives. Thus we get the conclusion that Calvin never shrank from affirming: even if the directive issued by some government official is morally reprehensible, if the official is the legitimate occupant of his office and is officially entitled to issue the directive, then we, the citizens, are obligated to obey. The directive generates in us the obligation to obey.

I have argued that this traditional line of thought is mistaken in its interpretation of Paul and confused in the conclusions it draws. The concept of authority that Paul employs is not that of positional authority but that of performance-authority. When it is taken all by itself, out of context, it's not implausible to interpret the third clause in verse 1, "those authorities that exist have been instituted by God," as teaching that those who legitimately occupy positions of authority have been placed in those positions by God; and it is then not implausible to interpret Paul as teaching, in the first clause, that it's because God has placed them in their positions that everybody is to "be subject to the governing authorities." If one then allows this interpretation of the opening verse to govern one's interpretation of the entire passage, one emerges with the traditional interpretation.

I have argued that the first verse should not be interpreted in isolation but in the light of Paul's more expansive comments in verses 4–6. In those verses Paul clearly teaches that God has authorized government to do certain things, and that when it does what it is divinely authorized to do, we must for that reason "be subject, not only because of wrath but also because of conscience."

Interpreting verse 1 as alluding to this teaching is easy and plausible whereas it is impossible to interpret verses 4–6 as operating with the concept of positional authority.

The confusion in the traditional line of thought lies in assuming that if some government official has positional authority to issue some directive to the public, then his doing so generates in the public the moral obligation to obey. We have seen that this assumption is false. The public may be *legally* obligated to obey. But a directive generates in them a moral obligation to obey only if it was morally permissible for the official to issue that directive.

This is not the end of the matter, however. Even if the directive does not generate in me the obligation to obey, it may nonetheless be the case that I should obey, perhaps even that I am obligated to obey. In deciding whether or not to obey one must take into account not only whether the directive did or did not generate in one an obligation to obey but also prudential and consequentialist considerations. One must take into account, for example, the likely consequences for the state's justice system as a whole of disobedience and non-submission by oneself and others. In some cases one may judge that disobedience or non-submission is likely to jolt the state into mending its ways; that would be a good reason for disobeying or not submitting. In other cases one may judge that disobedience or non-submission by oneself and others is likely to have the opposite effect, of seriously impairing the workings of the state's justice system, even of bringing about its collapse. Then one has to ask whether, all things considered, that would be a good thing or a bad thing, whether it would eventuate in greater justice overall or in greater injustice overall. And throughout all of these reflections one has to keep in mind the possibility that though it would be *prima facie* wrong to do to another what the state is ordering one to do, it would not be wrong all things considered.

CHAPTER 11

The political implications of the nature and existence of the church

I have insisted on the importance of locating our theologico-philosophical reflections on the state within the context of attention to governance-authority structures in general; at the same time I have emphasized how unusual a governance-authority structure the state is. In this chapter I will take note of how distinctive is that entity which is the Christian church, and draw out some of the political implications of its distinct feature. Thereby we will achieve some understanding of the duality of Christians being under the authority of both church and state.

In Chapter 8 we took note of various silences in Paul's discussion of government, the absence of answers to questions that we have. Among Paul's silences is silence on the relation of the church to the state. What I will be doing in this chapter is filling in his silence on this point, saying on his behalf what he did not say.

Given Paul's view of the church and what he knew about the Roman Empire, we know in advance that he would never have said that it was the God-given task of the empire to cultivate virtue and piety in its citizens. Would he have trusted your and my state to do that? Not a chance. But let's go beyond this obvious point.

Paul's mystical experience on the road to Damascus not only converted him from being a persecutor of the followers of Jesus to becoming one of them; it impelled him to preach the gospel to the Gentile world. In doing so he was carrying out the command issued by Jesus to the apostles upon his departure: "go and make disciples of all nations, baptizing them in the name of the Father and of the Son and of the Holy Spirit, and teaching them to obey everything that I have commanded you" (Matthew 28:19).

Many people in the cities in which Paul preached ignored what he had to say; others flat-out rejected it. But in every city, small groups accepted his message, acknowledged Jesus as Lord and Savior, were baptized, and began to assemble together to worship God, remember Jesus, and listen to scripture. They were united in fragile and imperfect, though nonetheless real, bonds of charity. In short, in response to the preaching of Paul and others a new religious community came into existence, under their noses, as it were.

Note well that a new religious community came into existence. The aim and result of Paul's teaching was not the introduction of some new religious practices and a new religious outlook, these to be added to the mix already present in the empire. The aim and result of his teaching was the creation of the church. He did not write tracts expounding something called "Christianity"; he wrote letters to the churches. Of course his readers did adopt new religious practices and did embrace a new religious outlook; but they did so in the context of confessing that Jesus was Lord and Savior, of being baptized, and of participating in the assemblies. In his letters we observe Paul struggling to understand and guide this new community that was coming into existence as the result of his endeavors and those of others.

The church is born, he says, not of the flesh but of the Spirit. The people who came together as the church in Corinth, for example, had not discovered some natural affinity for each other, had not learned of some shared occupation, plight, or project, had not discovered that they shared certain religious interests. Their affirmative response to the good news of the gospel, when others rejected it or were indifferent, was the work of the Holy Spirit. And the Spirit blows where it wills. We don't understand how it works.[1]

They were united in their declaration that Jesus was the Christ, the Messiah – their Lord and Savior. For them, the import of their participation in the liturgy was that this was their liturgical remembering of Jesus and the liturgical expression of their conviction that God in Christ was their Lord and Savior. This represented a certain interiorizing – dangerous word! Going through the motions of the liturgy means nothing. It does not placate God. The critique of sacrifices found in the Old Testament prophets was appropriated by the church. Sacrifice, said the prophets, is to be the expression of devotion; where devotion is missing, forget the sacrifices. Going through the motions nauseates God.[2]

We saw in Polycarp the fateful implications, for the relation of the members of the church to the emperor and his deputies, of their declaration that Christ was their Lord and King. That declaration implied that they did not view themselves as a group of people with spiritual needs who had banded together to form an organization for the purpose of conducting religious activities so

---

[1] John Courtney Murray, in *We Hold These Truths: Catholic Reflections on the American Proposition* (1960; reprinted Lanham, MD: Rowman & Littlefield, 2005), states the contrast nicely: "What is the Church? Is it a human thing, the work of man himself? Or is it a divine gift to man – not a 'gathered' but a 'given' Church?" (125).

[2] Compare the following passage from the early Church Father Lactantius: "[N]othing is so much a matter of free will as religion. The worship of God ... requires full commitment [*maximam devotionem*] and faith. For how will God love the worshipper if He Himself is not loved by him, or grant to the petitioner whatever he asks when he draws near and offers his prayer without sincerity [*ex animo*] or reverence. But they [the pagans], when they come to offer sacrifice, offer to their gods nothing from within, nothing of themselves, no innocence of mind, no reverence, no awe." Lactantius, *Divine Institutes*, v.20. I thank Robert Louis Wilken for the translation.

as to satisfy those needs. Their declaration was a political statement on their part; they acknowledged Christ as their sovereign.
Yet in spite of acknowledging Christ as their sovereign, they were
not a political movement. They made no attempt to set up a civil
government of their own, either within the empire or outside it.
Paul instructed them to live within the extant political structures as
peaceably as conscience permitted.

One more point requires emphasis. Paul and his fellow apostles
were adamant that confessing Christ as Lord and Savior, thereby
becoming a member of the church, meant that one had to
renounce all other religious affiliations; this new identity could
not simply be added on. Polycarp's declaration that Christ was his
King and Savior made him refuse to swear by the *tyché* of the
emperor. The church rejected syncretism.

In my description of the emergence of this new entity, the
church, I have used Pauline categories. Over the course of the
centuries other ways of understanding the church have been
developed. As we shall see in the next chapter, the "two rules"
doctrine concerning the relation between church and state, dominant in the West for many centuries, presupposed a different
understanding. I judge that today the Pauline understanding, as
one might call it, is once again dominant. But in any case, if we are
going to fill in Paul's silence on the relation between church and
state – say on his behalf what he did not say – it is this understanding that we must employ.

Let us now look at what happens when the church, so understood, spreads across the world. As the apostles went into all
nations, the effect was always the same: some people accepted
Christ as Lord and Savior and joined the church; others declined
or refused. The church was thus a foreign body in every nation in
which it emerged. On the one hand, its membership included

people from other nations; on the other hand, its membership never included all from any nation. The church included more than Romans but not all Romans; the church is not Roman. The church included more than Slavs but not all Slavs; the church is not Slavic. The church includes more than Americans but not all Americans; the church is not American. And so forth, for all nations, all peoples. The church is not the church *of* any nation or people. It does not belong to the social identity of any natural people.

By virtue of being a foreign body in the two ways mentioned, and by virtue of its rejection of syncretism, the church either produces or increases religious fissure in every society in which it emerges. If the society was religiously unified before, it is now no longer unified. Christians, in collusion with political regimes, have often acted as if this were not true. They have forced all citizens to be baptized on the assumption that that made them members of the church, forgetting or rejecting Paul's teaching that whereas the church is born of the Spirit, coercion is a work of the flesh. Or they have demanded that all citizens affirm "Christian principles," forgetting that the most fundamental principle the church affirms is that Christ is Lord and Savior and that those who make that affirmation are to be baptized and participate in the assemblies where God is worshipped, Jesus remembered, and scripture read.

There's another aspect to the universality of the church that requires mention, in addition to its transnationality, namely, its social universality. No natural features are required for being a member and participating in the life of the church, none at all. No racial identity is required, no gender, no sexual orientation, no ethnicity, no social class, nothing of the sort. Historically the church has found it extremely difficult to accept this social universality; often it has deliberately rejected it. But when it does decide to exclude some, it usually offers excuses, thereby betraying that it knows better.

The implication for the state of the religious fissure in its citizenry produced by the presence of the church is that the state cannot express the shared religious identity of the people, since there is no such identity. The coming of the church undermines the political vision of the ancient philosophers, that government is the highest institutional expression of the religio-ethical bonds uniting the citizens. Wherever the church enters a society, it destroys whatever religio-ethical unity that society may have possessed. Now there is only religious pluralism. The church has sometimes used coercion in an attempt to prevent this pluralism; in doing so, it has acted contrary to its own nature.

A persistent lament in the writings of traditionalists and conservatives in recent years, both Christian and non-Christian, is that the polity of a liberal democratic state rejects in principle the project of giving political expression to a shared religio-moral vision and that, on that account, it lacks a moral basis for its structure and actions. Rather than being the political expression of a community with a shared religio-moral vision, it is at best an association of such communities, a way of getting along, a *modus vivendi*. As such it is bound to become purely utilitarian, bureaucratic, and technocratic. It cannot long endure.

It's a strange lament for Christians to sound. The coming of the church into a society destroys whatever religious unity the society might previously have had and does not replace it with another.

The very nature of the church, when understood along Pauline lines, thus has implications for the kind of state that the church will pray for, hope for, struggle for, and insist on wherever it finds itself. There are general principles of justice that Christians do or should accept that can be employed to argue for conclusions identical with, or closely similar to, these implications; but more basic than constructing arguments employing such principles is recognizing the political implications of the nature and existence of that particular entity which is the church.

(1) The church will seek freedom from interference by the state in its governance and in its performance of those activities that constitute the life of the church; it will seek autonomy vis-à-vis the state, institutional freedom. Over and over governments have tried to exercise control over the church; they view an autonomous church as a nuisance if not a menace. The very nature of the church leads its members, or should lead its members, to resist all such interference. The church is not a creature of the state; it is born of the Spirit. Authorization to do and say what it does do and say is conferred upon it by Christ, not by the state. Its pastors are commissioned by Christ, not by the state; the authority they exercise has not been delegated to them by the state. With respect to every state, the church is always *there already*, doing what it is authorized to do. It does not await authorization by the state.

(2) The church will insist that the state allow it the freedom to invite those who are not members to join, and allow those who want to join the freedom to do so. And it will insist that the state allow those who do not want to join the freedom not to do so.

(3) The church will insist that the state allow the church the freedom to induct children of members of the church into the confessions and life of the church.

(4) The church will insist that the state allow its members the freedom to engage in those activities that are the life of the

church – publicly confessing Jesus as Lord and Savior, being baptized, attending the assemblies in which God is worshipped, Christ remembered, and scripture read. But it will likewise insist that the state not coerce any citizens into participating in the activities that are the life of the church. For, to say it once again, the church is born not of the flesh but of the Spirit.

(5) The church will insist that the state not force its members to do anything that they regard as compromising their declaration that Christ is their Lord and Savior. And if the state does try to coerce them into performing any such compromising act as swearing by the *tychê* of the emperor, they will refuse.

(6) The church will insist that the state not coerce its members, in their daily lives, to act contrary to what Christ commanded.

These six principles together constitute an expansive charter for the autonomy of the church vis-à-vis the state and for the religious freedom of citizens in general – or to put it from the opposite side, an expansive set of limits on what the state may do with respect to the church, its members, and citizens in general. What the church asks of the state is not merely that the church be given the freedom to sponsor Christian "religious activities" and that citizens be given the freedom to participate in such activities. It asks of the state the freedom to be that peculiar kind of community which is the church.

The fact that the presence of the church in some society makes it impossible for the state to be the highest institutional expression of the shared religious identity of the people, since there is no such identity to be expressed, leaves it open for the state to express the religious identity of just some of its citizens. That happens all the time. Present-day Israel identifies itself as a Jewish state; a good many states in the contemporary world identify themselves as Muslim states; and though the United States does not identify itself as a Christian state, a number of Americans insist that it was once a Christian state and should become that again.

Sometimes such governmental partiality takes the form of the state, in its distribution of benefits, favoring those who are of the preferred religion. The favoring need not be inscribed in law; those not of the favored religion may find that though they are not legally excluded from receiving certain benefits, those benefits are so intimately entangled with the preferred religion that they would compromise themselves if they accepted them. This was often the situation of the early Christians with respect to the Roman Empire. Sometimes such partiality takes the form of the state requiring that one be of the preferred religion to hold certain governmental offices. Sometimes it takes the form of the state itself sponsoring religious activities, as when the United States government hires chaplains. Let us call all such forms of partiality on the part of the state, *preferential establishment of religion.*

Some preferential establishment of religion is innocuous. It is probably innocuous that the United States Senate has a chaplain who offers prayers at the opening of sessions; it is probably innocuous that the English monarch must be a member of the Anglican Church. But when the church understands itself along the lines I have suggested, it will, in general, cast a suspicious eye on preferential establishment of religion. For preferential establishment of religion typically puts pressure on citizens to join the church and participate in its activities, or puts pressure on citizens not to do so. The church is opposed to pressure of both forms.

Once one notes that the nature and existence of the church imply the autonomy of the church vis-à-vis the state and the freedom of citizens to join or not to join, the question comes immediately to mind, what about the corresponding freedom of citizens to be Jews, Muslims, Hindus, Buddhists, atheists, and so forth? Will the church be indifferent to their freedom or lack thereof? When the church speaks to the state, will it ask only for its own institutional autonomy and only for the freedom of citizens to join or not join the church?

It will not. The insistence of the church that the state grant its citizens the freedom to join the church and share in its confession and activities, coupled with the opposition of the church to syncretism, implies that the church will be opposed to the state's putting pressure on anyone to participate in some religion other than Christianity. The issue that remains is, what about the state's putting pressure on its citizens *not* to participate in *some* of the other religions? The church will oppose the state's putting pressure on its citizens *not* to participate in *any* of the other religions; that would be tantamount to coercing them into either going through the motions of being a member of the church or into being overtly nonreligious, should that option remain open. But what about the state pressuring them *not* to participate in *certain* of the other religions?

So far as I can see, the existence and nature of the church have no implications, one way or the other, on this issue. What is relevant instead is the commitment of the church to justice. It would be unjust for the state to grant to the church the freedom I described while denying the counterpart freedom to others. The church will be of the conviction that some of the actions of those others amount to wronging God; but an implication of the principle just suggested is that the church will insist that those others have the political right to wrong God in those ways. This is another application of a principle that we took note of in Chapter 8:

though the state is assigned the task of curbing wrongdoing, it cannot curb all incidents of wrongdoing, and there are some forms of wrongdoing that it should not try to curb. The consequence of doing so would be that the state itself becomes a perpetrator of serious wrongdoing.

If the nature and existence of the church, plus the principle of justice just now enunciated, do indeed have the political implications that I have set forth, then anyone who is a member of the church will insist that government lacks authority to infringe on the freedoms mentioned. The situation is not that government has the authority to infringe on those freedoms but ought not to do so; the situation is that it exceeds its authority if it does so. At some times and in some places the church will, of course, get nowhere in its insistence on these forms of freedom; at other times and in other places it will, along with other religious communities, enjoy some of these freedoms and not others. And if in some times and places the members of the church operate with a different understanding of the church from that which I have articulated, they may be content with only some of these freedoms; they may even collude with the state in its infringement on some of them.

In our discussion in Chapter 7 I quoted Calvin as saying that it is among the "appointed" ends of civil government to "cherish and protect the outward worship of God, [and] to defend sound' doctrine of piety and the position of the church." I might have quoted Aquinas to substantially the same effect. Here is what Aquinas says in book I, chapter xv of his small tract *On Princely Government* (*De regimine principum*):

Because the end of our living well at this present time is the blessedness of heaven, the king's duty is therefore to secure the good life for the community in such a way as to ensure that it is led to the blessedness of heaven, that is, by commanding those things which conduce to the blessedness of heaven and forbidding, as far as it is possible to do so, those which are contrary.[3]

Paul says nothing that remotely resembles these declarations by Calvin and Aquinas. Assuming that Paul's understanding of the church was substantially that which I have presented, his silence on this point was as significant as silence can be. Government has no authority to do what Calvin and Aquinas say it ought to do. It's obvious that Paul did not think that it was within the authority of the *Roman Empire* to do what Aquinas and Calvin say government should do. But our discussion in this chapter leads us to conclude that only if the church misunderstands its own nature will it ever ask government to do what Calvin and Aquinas say it should do. Let alone asking government to do these things, the church will not *willingly accede* to government doing them. The nature and existence of the church drastically limit the scope of governmental authority.

In his well-known essay of 1938 "Church and State,"[4] Karl Barth posed the question, "Is there a connection between justification of the sinner through faith alone, completed once for all by God through Jesus Christ, and the problem of justice, the problem of human law? Is there an inward and vital connection?" (101). He went on to say that exploring the connection between justice and justification is only one way of approaching the topic he had in mind. One might also approach it using *order* as one's main concept, or *peace*, *freedom*, or *service*. What, for example, is the connection

---

[3] *St Thomas Aquinas: Political Writings*, trans. and ed. R. W. Dyson (Cambridge University Press, 2002), p. 53.

[4] The essay is to be found in the collection Karl Barth, *Community, State, and Church* (Garden City, NY: Anchor Books, Doubleday & Co., 1960), pp. 101–48. References are incorporated into the text.

between "what we are accustomed to call 'Divine Service' in the worship of the Church as such, and another form of service, what may be described as a 'political' service of God" (101–02)?

Barth went on to observe that the tradition of Reformation theology fails us here; no doubt he was of the same view concerning traditional Catholic theology. The Reformers clearly and powerfully emphasized "that both realities exist: divine justification and human justice, the proclamation of Jesus Christ, faith in Him and the office and authority of the secular power, the mission of the Church and the mission of the State, the hidden life of the Christian in God and also his duty as a citizen" (102). The Reformers "took great pains to make it clear that the two are not in conflict, but that they can very well exist side by side, each being competent in its own sphere" (102). But there they dropped the discussion, when what we need to know is "not only that the two are not in conflict, but, first and foremost, to what extent they are connected."

In short, it was Barth's view that there is a big "gap" at this point in the theological tradition which we "can neither overlook nor take lightly." We cannot be content to think that "human justice [is] merely clamped on to the truth of divine justification, instead of being vitally connected with it" (102). The ever-present danger, when one's teaching on justice is allowed to sit side by side, un-integrated, with one's teaching on justification, is that either one's teaching on justification becomes a purely spiritual message or one's teaching on justice becomes purely secular. To prevent these "sterile and dangerous separations" (105) we must ask, "is there an actual, and therefore inward and vital, connection between the two realms?" (106). We cannot be content with merely distinguishing them.

In this chapter I have done what Barth urged; I have explored the implications of the nature and existence of the church for the scope of the state's authority. What emerged was a state distinctly limited in its authority with respect to the church and religion: the state is to grant institutional autonomy to the church and to all other counterpart religious institutions, and it is to grant religious freedom to all citizens.

As I mentioned above, conclusions very much like the ones I have reached could also be reached by appealing to principles of justice; if I were addressing those who have no interest in the political implications of the nature and existence of the church, that's how I would conduct the discussion.[5] But here I am addressing those interested in Christian political theology. For Christians, even more fundamental than asking what justice requires is uncovering the political implications of the very nature and existence of that unique entity which is the church.

The *Declaration on Religious Freedom* issued by Pope Paul VI at the close of the Second Vatican Council took the other path to the conclusions we have reached, the path that appeals to principles of justice. The *Declaration* says that to restrict someone's religious freedom is to violate his or her dignity as a person: "the right to religious freedom is based on the very dignity of the human person ... not in the subjective attitude of the individual but in his very nature."[6] The *Declaration* goes on to argue for the

---

[5] It is remarkable that the second-century Church Father Tertullian already argued that justice requires freedom of religious exercise – or more precisely, that natural right does. Here is what he says: "It is a human law and a natural right [*naturalis potestatis*] that one should worship whatever he intends [*quod putaverit colere*]; the religious practice of one person neither harms nor helps another. It is no part of religion to coerce religious practice, for it is by free choice not coercion that we should be led to religion [*nec religionis est cogere religionem, quae sponte suscipi debeat, non vi*]." Tertullian, *Ad Scapulam*, 2.1–2. I thank Robert Louis Wilken for the translation.

[6] *Dignitatis humanae*, ¶2. Quotation from *Vatican Council II: The Conciliar and Post-Conciliar Documents*, ed. Austin Flannery, OP (Northport, NY: Costello Publishing Co., 1975).

institutional autonomy of the church and other such religious communities. "Religious communities are a requirement of the social nature of man and of religion itself." They "have a right to immunity so that they may organize themselves according to their own principles. They must be allowed to honor the Supreme Godhead with public worship, help their members to practice their religion and strengthen them, with religious instruction, and promote institutions in which members may work together to organize their own lives according to their religious principles." These communities "also have the right not to be hindered by legislation or administrative action on the part of the civil authority in the selection, training, appointment, and transferal of their own ministers, in communicating with religious authorities and communities in other parts of the world, in erecting buildings for religious purposes, and in the acquisition and use of the property they need."[7]

The affirmation of these principles by Vatican II represented a remarkable shift in the views of the Catholic Church concerning religious freedom and the relation between church and state. In place of its traditional perfectionist view, succinctly expressed by Aquinas in the passage quoted above, it now affirms a protectionist view: religious communities *have a right to immunity*. By all accounts it was the American Catholic theologian John Courtney Murray who played the decisive role in the shift; Murray argued that the Catholic Church should take note of the American experience and not forever be haunted by the French Revolution.[8]

---

[7] *Dignitatis humanae*, ¶4.

[8] It is worth noting, however, that in *We Hold These Truths*, Murray defends the religion clauses of the First Amendment to the United States Constitution on consequentialist grounds rather than on justice grounds; he calls them "articles of peace." "If history makes one thing clear," he says, "it is that these clauses were the twin children of social

I affirm the philosophico-theological line of argument in the *Declaration on Religious Freedom*. But the path I have taken in this chapter to these same conclusions is a different path, a path less traveled, indeed seldom traveled, a path that starts not from principles of justice but from the nature and existence of that unique social entity which is the church.

necessity, the necessity of creating a social environment, protected by law, in which men of different religious faiths might live together in peace" (69). He goes on to say that "in regarding the religion clauses of the First Amendment as articles of peace and in placing the case for them on the primary grounds of their social necessity, one is not taking low ground. Such a case does not appeal to mean-spirited expediency ... In the science of law and the art of jurisprudence the appeal to social peace is an appeal to a high moral value. Behind the will to social peace there stands a divine and Christian imperative. This is the classic and Christian tradition" (71).

CHAPTER 12

Discarding the "two rules" doctrine

In a letter of 494 to the Emperor Anastasius, Pope Gelasius I declared that "two there are, august Emperor, by which this world is ruled: the consecrated authority of priests and the royal power." The idea that Gelasius here expresses is that pope and emperor, church and state are distinct authority structures whose essential difference is that they have jurisdiction over two distinct domains of human activity. In his tract of two years later, *On the Bond of Anathema*, Gelasius elaborated the idea. Church and empire each have a distinct "sphere of competence," a distinct "jurisdiction." Christ himself, says Gelasius, "made a distinction between the two rules, assigning each its sphere of operation and its due respect." The emperor has governance over "human" or "secular" affairs. The pope, along with his bishops and priests, have governance over "divine affairs," over "spiritual activity."[1]

The doctrine that Gelasius articulated in these passages came to be known as the "two rules" doctrine. From the time he wrote his letter until a century or so after the Protestant Reformation, the framework employed for discussing the relation between church and state, and the relation of Christians to these two entities, was

---

[1] My quotations from Gelasius are all from the translations to be found in Oliver O'Donovan and Joan Lockwood O'Donovan, eds. and trans., *From Irenaeus to Grotius: A Sourcebook in Christian Political Thought 100–1625* (Grand Rapids: Wm. B. Eerdmans Publishing Co., 1999), pp. 178–79.

almost always the "two rules" doctrine. John Courtney Murray describes the doctrine as "Christianity's cardinal contribution to the Western political tradition."[2] With the "two rules" doctrine we are, he says, "in the presence of a Great Idea, whose entrance into history marked the beginning of a new civilizational era."[3] The doctrine rejected "the classical view of society as a single homogeneous structure, within which the political power stood forth as the representative of society both in its religious and in its political aspects. Augustus was both *Summus Imperator* and *Pontifex Maximus*."[4] What must be added is that, though the doctrine shaped almost all discussions about church and state for a millennium, in practice it was almost always being egregiously violated somewhere or other.[5]

My discussion in the preceding chapter, of the political implications of the nature and existence of the church, implies that the "two rules" doctrine must be rejected as a way of understanding the duality of Christians being under the authority of both church and state. The church does indeed *have* a governance-authority structure – or rather, given the highly fractured condition of the church, it has a multiplicity of governance-authority structures. But the church as such is not a governance-authority structure.

---

[2] John Courtney Murray, *We Hold These Truths: Catholic Reflections on the American Proposition* (1960; reprinted Lanham, MD: Rowman & Littlefield, 2005), p. 75.

[3] Ibid., p. 187.   [4] Ibid.

[5] The standard documentary history of the conflict between church and state is Sidney Z. Ehler and John B. Morrall, trans. and eds., *Church and State through the Centuries: A Collection of Historic Documents with Commentaries* (New York: Biblo and Tannen, 1967). Sidney Z. Ehler's *Twenty Centuries of Church and State: A Survey of their Relations in Past and Present* (Westminster, MD: Newman Press, 1957) is a less detailed telling of the story. Brian Tierney's *The Crisis of Church and State: 1050–1300: With Selected Documents* (Englewood Cliffs, NJ: Prentice-Hall, 1964; reprinted University of Toronto Press, 1988) fills in the details for the medieval period. There is at yet no comparable detailed and comprehensive history for the Reformation period. (I owe these references to John Witte.)

It is a community, a transnational people of an unusual sort, "a holy nation" in the words of 1 Peter 2:9. Church and state are entities of two fundamentally different ontological types.

It would be a mistake, however, to discard the "two rules" doctrine for this reason and say nothing more about it. Given the prominence of the doctrine in the tradition, it's important that we take time to understand just what it affirmed and why, and to probe more deeply why it must be rejected.

Let's have before us a fleshed-out articulation of the doctrine. Once again I turn to Calvin; his articulation of the doctrine is as good as any and better than most. Here is his statement of what he calls "twofold government":

Let us ... consider that there is a twofold government in man; one aspect is spiritual, whereby the conscience is instructed in piety and in reverencing God, the second political, whereby man is educated for the duties of humanity and citizenship that must be maintained among men. These are usually called the "spiritual" and the "temporal" jurisdiction (not improper terms) by which is meant that the former sort of government pertains to the life of the soul, while the latter has to do with the concerns of the present life – not only with food and clothing but with laying down laws whereby a man may live his life among other men holily, honorably, and temperately. For the former resides in the inner mind, while the latter regulates only outward behavior. The one we may call the spiritual kingdom, the other, the political kingdom. (*Institutes*, III.xix.15)[6]

---

[6] I am using the translation by Ford Lewis Battles, *Institutes of the Christian Religion* (Philadelphia: Westminster Press, 1950). References are incorporated into the text. Here is how Hugh of St. Victor put it, writing more or less midway between Gelasius and Calvin: "There are two lives, one earthly, the other heavenly, one corporeal, the other spiritual ... Each has its own good by which it is invigorated and nourished ... Therefore, in each ... life, powers were established ... The one power is therefore called secular, the other spiritual ... The earthly power has as its head the king. The spiritual power has as its head the supreme pontiff. All things that are earthly and made for the earthly life belong to the power of the king. All things that are spiritual and attributed to the spiritual life belong to the power of the supreme pontiff." *De sacramentis christianae fidei* (ca. 1134), quoted by Stephen D. Smith, *The Disenchantment of Secular Discourse* (Cambridge, MA: Harvard University Press, 2010), p. 117.

Calvin is emphatic, aggressive even, in his insistence on the importance of distinguishing these two modes of governance. "These two, as we have divided them, must always be examined separately; and while one is being considered, we must call away and turn aside the mind from thinking about the other. There are in man, so to speak, two worlds, over which different kings and different laws have authority" (ibid.). One could not ask for a more clear and forceful statement of what Barth found objectionable in traditional discussions of church and state.

When Calvin turns to the topic of church discipline in the *Institutes*, IV.xi, he says that the disciplinary aspect

> of ecclesiastical power [is] the most important in a well-ordered state. This [aspect] consists of jurisdiction. But the whole jurisdiction of the church pertains to the discipline of morals ... For as no city or township can function without magistrate and polity, so the church of God ... needs a spiritual polity. This is, however, quite distinct from the civil polity, yet does not hinder or threaten it but rather greatly helps and furthers it. (IV.xi.1)

Calvin then elaborates the "difference and unlikeness there is between ecclesiastical and civil power" as follows:

> The church does not have the right of the sword to punish or compel, not the authority to force; not imprisonment, nor the other punishments which the magistrate commonly inflicts. Then, it is not a question of punishing the sinner against his will, but of the sinner professing his repentance in a voluntary chastisement. The two conceptions are very different ... An example will make this clearer. Suppose a man is drunk. In a well-ordered city, imprisonment will be the penalty. Suppose he is a fornicator. His punishment will be similar or, rather, greater. So will the laws, the magistrate, and outward justice be satisfied. Yet he may happen to show no sign of repentance, but, rather, murmur or grumble. Shall the church stop there? Such men cannot be received to the Lord's Supper. (IV.xi.3)

Recall, from our discussion in Chapter 7, Calvin's general statement concerning the jurisdiction of civil government: "civil government has as its appointed end ... to cherish and protect the outward worship of God, to defend sound doctrine of piety and the position of the church, to adjust our life to the society of men, to form our social behavior to civil righteousness, to reconcile us with one another, and to promote general peace and tranquility."

You and I, reading this passage and others like it more than four centuries after Calvin wrote them, find this way of thinking not only objectionable but strange and alien. As citizens of liberal democracies we reject Calvin's declaration that it is the business of civil government to cherish and protect the outward worship of God and defend sound doctrine of piety and the position of the church. But beyond that, we find the distinction that he employs problematic, the distinction between cultivating and coercing pious and virtuous *outward behavior* and cultivating piety and virtue in the *inner mind*. The distinction seems to us obscure and fraught with difficulties; we no longer think in these terms. Here, especially, what Lilla says about political theology in general applies: "we are puzzled, since we have only a distant memory of what it was like to think" this way. "We live, so to speak, on the other shore."

Calvin was probably familiar with every difficulty posed by the distinction that you and I might think of, along with a good many others that don't occur to us because we have not been forced, as he was, to deal with ambiguous cases.[7] Yet the difficulty in drawing the distinction between the inner spiritual and the outer temporal, and the consequent difficulty in distinguishing between

---

[7] David Van Drunen, in *Natural Law and the Two Kingdoms: A Study in the Development of Reformed Social Thought* (Grand Rapids: Wm. B. Eerdmans Publishing Co., 2010), pp. 82–86, points not just to the haziness of the distinction but to inconsistencies between Calvin's theory and his practice in Geneva.

the jurisdiction of the church and the jurisdiction of the state, did not lead Calvin to give up this way of thinking; neither did it lead others to give it up. So what was it that led him and almost everybody else to think along these lines in spite of the difficulty of drawing the distinction between the two jurisdictions?

Clues to the answer are to be found in the passages I quoted. Gelasius spoke of those by whom "this world" is ruled. Calvin says that "in man" government is twofold; in one form, "the conscience" is trained in piety and divine worship, in the other, "the individual" is instructed in civil duties. In the former, "the soul" is instructed; in the latter, "outward behavior" is regulated.

Gelasius and Calvin treated the membership of the church as coterminous with the citizenry of the state. In describing the different jurisdictions of church and state, neither Gelasius nor Calvin says, or even suggests, that their jurisdictions differ with respect to those who fall under their jurisdictions. Gelasius would have known of the presence of Jews here and there within the empire; Calvin would have known of the presence of Jews within the governmental jurisdictions of his day. But the presence of the Jews was treated as an anomaly; it did not provoke rethinking. As for those who had been excommunicated, whether for heresy or scandalous behavior, they remained members of the church. Not members in "good standing," of course, but members nonetheless. Excommunication barred them from "communicating" at the sacrament of Holy Communion; it did not remove them from membership in the church.[8]

---

[8] Bruce Gordon, in his biography of Calvin titled *Calvin* (New Haven: Yale University Press, 2009), says that "To Calvin's great satisfaction, in 1541 the Genevan council created parishes in which every person was to be baptized, receive the Lord's Supper and learn the catechism" (127). He also remarks that "For Calvin, God's Church on earth included all people, the faithful and the reprobate" (134).

Suppose that this is how one thinks. And suppose the question then arises of the relationship between church and state. Already by the time of Gelasius conflicts between pope and emperor made it impossible to think of church and state as identical. With that option eliminated, it's hard to see any other answer on the horizon than that of the "two rules" doctrine: church and state are distinct authority structures, distinguished by the different activities over which they have jurisdiction. There is no difference in the *scope* of their jurisdiction; they have jurisdiction over exactly, or almost exactly, the same human beings. The difference lies in the *domain* of their jurisdiction; they have jurisdiction over different domains, different dimensions, different aspects, of the life of the people. The traditional way of drawing that distinction in jurisdiction was hazy, but not flat-out implausible: the church deals with spiritual matters, the state with secular matters, the church with heavenly matters, the state with temporal matters, the church with inward piety and virtue, the state with outward behavior.[9] Once one has said or assumed that the membership of the church is coterminous with the citizenry of the state, one has made it impossible to think of the church along the lines laid out in the preceding chapter, namely, as the people of God present in every nation but identical with none.

Be it noted, however, that from the doctrine that the difference between church and state is a difference in the activities over which they have jurisdiction, it does not follow that "two there are ... by which this world is ruled," or, to use Calvin's words, "that man is under a twofold government." In earlier chapters of this essay I took note of the fact that society is pervaded by a

---

[9] Calvin and many other writers were well aware of the fact that the idea of one society under two rules, one religious and one political, goes back to ancient Israel, where the priesthood was distinct from the monarchy.

multiplicity and variety of governance-authority structures; I located our discussion of the authority of the state within that context. It may well be true that the number and variety of distinct governance-authority structures is much larger in modern Western society than it was in the late antique society of Gelasius or in Calvin's sixteenth-century society. But in Calvin's day there were guilds, distinct from both church and state; and both in Gelasius' society and in Calvin's there were families. So why did the writers in that long tradition of Christian political thought not open their discussions by first noting, as we did, that there are many ways in which humankind is governed, and then declaring that they wished to discuss the relation between the two of these that (in their view) have governance over everybody?

I do not know the answer to this question; perhaps somewhere in the work of historians there is an answer. What should be noted, however, is that the failure to establish, as the context for one's discussion, the multiplicity and variety of governance-authority structures is not innocuous; it invites us either to ignore those other structures or, if we do take note of them, to think of them all as somehow deriving their authority from either church or state.

Nobody any longer thinks of the relation between church and state in terms of the "two rules" doctrine. Once most people did; now nobody does. Between them and us an enormous alteration of mentality has taken place. The reason is obvious. It has become impossible for us to think of the membership of the church in some area as coterminous with the citizenry of the state that has jurisdiction over that area – impossible for us to think of the membership of the church in the United States as coterminous with the American citizenry. Not only is the church now fractured into denominations, and beyond that, into so-called *independent churches*; present among us are Jews, Muslims, Buddhists, Hindus, explicit atheists, and so forth. We can, if we wish, compare the effectuation of God's rule that takes place in states with the effectuation of God's rule that takes place in the churches; and we can look for commonalities in how the effectuation of God's rule takes place within the churches. But we can no longer think of church and state as two modes of the effectuation of God's rule over humankind in general.

An equally enormous change has taken place in how those of us who are citizens of rights-limited democracies think of the authority and task of the state. When you and I think about the authority of the state, we think immediately about *limits* on its authority – limits within the domain of "external behavior." The state exceeds its authority if it censors our public speech or imposes on us cruel and unusual punishment. It does not merely do what it ought not to do; it exceeds its authority. Calvin would agree that the state ought not to do these things; he would not agree that in doing these things it exceeds its authority.

The most common way of making our point is to say that citizens have a natural right to free speech, a natural right to freedom of religious exercise, a natural right not to be subjected to cruel and unusual punishment, and so on. The idea that citizens have certain natural rights, and that these rights impose limits on state authority, plays no systematic role in Calvin's thought whatsoever. In the thought of the first generation after Calvin it did play a systematic role.[10]

---

[10] For the story of how this went, see John Witte, *The Reformation of Rights: Law, Religion, and Human Rights in Early Modern Calvinism* (Cambridge University Press, 2007).

And not only do we, when thinking about the authority of the state, immediately think of its authority as limited by the rights of citizens; we also think differently about the *task* of the state from how traditional "two rules" thinkers thought about that task. The central task of the state was said to be to cultivate pious and virtuous behavior on the part of the citizens. The view of most of us comes closer to St Paul's view, that the central task of the state is to curb injustice.

Let me quote Calvin's most expansive statement on the task of government. Government, he says,

does not merely see to it ... that men breathe, eat, drink, and are kept warm, even though it surely embraces all these activities when it provides for their living together. It does not, I repeat, look to this only, but also prevents idolatry, sacrilege against God's name, blasphemies against his truth, and other public offenses against religion from arising and spreading among the people; it prevents the public peace from being disturbed, it provides that each man may keep his property safe and sound, that men may carry on blameless intercourse among themselves, that honesty and modesty may be preserved among men. In short, it provides that a public manifestation of religion may exist among Christians, and that humanity be maintained among men. (IV.xx.3)

There were people in Calvin's day arguing that civil government has no such duties with respect to religion. Calvin replies:

Let no man be disturbed that I now commit to civil government the duty of rightly establishing religion ... For, when I approve of a civil administration that aims to prevent the true religion which is contained in God's law from being openly and with public sacrilege violated and defiled with impunity, I do not here ... allow men to make laws according to their own decision concerning religion and the worship of God. (Ibid.)

Calvin does not here say that unity in religion among the citizenry is indispensable to the functioning and endurance of the state – though no doubt he believed it was. What he says is that among the laws God has issued to us are laws concerning religion and the worship of God; what he takes for granted is that it is the business of the state to encourage and coerce external conformity to God's laws in general. If some action is morally or religiously impermissible, then the state should not give its citizens the freedom to perform it. Wrongdoing should have no civil rights.

Essential to the emergence of the rights-limited state was the rejection of this principle by theorists and citizens alike. I may think your religion is wrong; but I will defend your civil right to be free to practice it.

I mentioned that nobody any longer thinks of the relation between church and state in terms of the "two rules" doctrine, the reason being that, in the modern Western world, it is patently obvious that the membership of the church in some area is not coterminous with the citizens of the state that has jurisdiction in that area. But from the fact that we no longer think in these terms it must not be inferred that this way of thinking has disappeared without a trace. It has not.

The basic affirmation of the "two rules" doctrine was that the church should be free of control by the state and the state should be free of control by the church. The doctrine articulated this affirmation in terms of the church and the state being two authority structures having authority over the same populace but with different jurisdictions. One can discard that way of articulating the affirmation without discarding the affirmation itself, that the church should be free of control by the state and that the state should be free of control by the church. The two religion clauses in the First Amendment to the United States Constitution should be understood as doing exactly that. The two clauses are an application of the fundamental affirmation of the "two rules" doctrine to the new situation of a religiously pluralistic society.

John Courtney Murray develops the point in *We Hold These Truths*.[11] "The American Constitution," he says, "embodies in a special way the traditional principle of the distinction between church and state" (77). "The American thesis is that government is not juridically omnipotent. Its powers are limited, and one of the principles of limitation is the distinction between state and church, in their purposes, methods, and manner of organization" (78). "Made autonomous in its own sphere, government was denied all competence in the field of religion. In this field freedom was to be the rule and method; government was powerless to legislate respecting an establishment of religion and likewise powerless to prohibit the free exercise of religion" (77).

It is commonly assumed that the "two kingdoms" doctrine of traditional Lutheranism is the same as what I have been calling, following common usage, the "two rules" doctrine. Whatever may be true of Lutheran writers generally, let me close this chapter by noting that early in his career Luther departed in significant ways from the long tradition of "two rules" thinking.

In his tract *Temporal Authority: To What Extent It Should Be Obeyed*,[12] Luther declares that:

All who are not Christians belong to the kingdom of the world and are under the law. There are few true believers, and still fewer who live a Christian life, who do not resist evil and indeed themselves do no evil. For this reason God has provided for them [i.e., non-Christians] a different government beyond the Christian estate and kingdom of God. (587)

---

[11] References to this book are hereafter incorporated into the text.
[12] I am using the translation in O'Donovan and O'Donovan, eds. and trans., *From Irenaeus to Grotius*.

After distinguishing between government as exercised by the state and government as exercised by the church, Luther then says that both forms of government

must be permitted to remain; the one to produce righteousness, the other to bring about external peace and prevent evil deeds. Neither one is sufficient in the world without the other. No one can become righteous in the sight of God by means of the temporal government, without Christ's spiritual government. Christ's government does not extend over all men; rather, Christians are always a minority in the midst of non-Christians. (Ibid.)

The membership of the church is not coterminous with the citizenry of the state.

A bit later in the tract Luther describes the domain of the state's jurisdiction: "The temporal government has laws which extend no further than to life and property and external affairs on earth, for God cannot and will not permit anyone but himself to rule over the soul. Therefore, where the temporal authority presumes to pre-scribe laws for the soul, it encroaches upon God's government and only misleads souls and destroys them" (591). There is nothing in this last passage that Calvin could not agree to. Not so for the following passage, in which Luther clarifies what he has in mind:

You say: "The temporal power is not forcing men to believe; it is simply seeing to it externally that no one deceives the people by false doctrine; how could heretics otherwise be restrained?" Answer: This the bishops should do; it is a function entrusted to them and not to the princes. Heresy can never be restrained by force. One will have to tackle the problem in some other way, for heresy must be opposed and dealt with otherwise than with the sword. Here God's word must do the fighting. If it does not succeed, certainly the temporal power will not succeed either, even if it were to drench the world in blood. Heresy is a spiritual matter which you cannot hack to pieces with iron, consume with fire, or drown in water. (502–03)

The understanding of the church that Luther presents in these passages, and his spelling-out of the limits that the nature and existence of the church, so understood, place on the state, is a striking departure from that presupposed in the traditional "two rules" doctrine. In its essentials it is the same as that which I presented in the preceding chapter.

The *Temporal Authority* tract was an early writing of Luther. As his career progressed, he increasingly reverted to the views of his predecessors and assigned to the state the task of supporting the church and cultivating external manifestations of piety.[13] In his early writings he anticipated the new relation between church and state that came to expression in the United States Bill of Rights; in his later writings, he backed off.

[13] See the discussion by the editors in O'Donovan and O'Donovan, eds. and trans., *From Irenaeus to Grotius*, p. 583.

CHAPTER 13

The rights-limited state

How did we get from there to here – from a time when almost all Christians in the West thought about the relation between church and state in terms of the "two rules" doctrine to now when nobody does? Let me quote a passage from a well-known pamphlet written in French that appeared in 1579, *A Discourse upon the Permission of Freedom of Religion, Called Religions-Vrede in the Netherlands.* Though the author presents himself as Catholic, the predominance of scholarly opinion nowadays is that he was the prominent Huguenot Philip du Plessis Mornay.

I ask those who do not want to admit the two religions in this country how they now intend to abolish one of them ... It goes without saying that you cannot abolish any religious practice without using force and taking up arms, and going to war against each other instead of taking up arms in unison against Don John and his adherents and delivering us from the insupportable tyranny of the foreigners. If we intend to ruin the Protestants we will ruin ourselves, as the French did. The conclusion to be drawn from this is that it would be better to live in peace with them, rather than ruin ourselves by internal discord and carry on a hazardous, disastrous, long and difficult war or rather a perpetual and impossible one. Taking everything into consideration, we can choose between two things: we can either allow them to live in peace with us or we can all die together; we can either let them be or, desiring to destroy them, be ourselves destroyed by their ruin ... As we cannot forbid these people to practise their religion without starting a war and cannot destroy them by that war without being destroyed ourselves let us conclude that we must let them live in peace and grant them liberty.[1]

The argument is eloquent and poignant. The situation in the Lowlands is that the religious unity that once prevailed is gone. Many have rejected the Catholic Church and become Protestant. Any attempt to recover the hegemony of the Catholic Church by force of arms would require appalling bloodshed, devastating not only the Protestant but also the Catholic population and leaving both at the mercy of the Spanish tyrant. The only option is to grant liberty to the Protestants, live at peace with them, and together fight Don John. It's an overtly consequentialist argument, close kin to the argument of John Courtney Murray that we took note of in the preceding chapter, that the religion clauses in the United States Bill of Rights are "articles of peace."

It was the impossibility of undoing the religious fission caused by the emergence of Protestantism that eventually forced European Christians to consider some form of political community alternative to Christendom and its "two rules" structure. Initially, as we know, they played with the idea of mini-Christendoms, each political unit enforcing its own preferred religion. But within a relatively short period even that project proved impossible. Northwest Europe was forced to take hesitant and tentative steps toward the rights-limited state in which the church is granted autonomy from state interference and in which individuals are granted the civil right to free exercise of their religion.

I want now to take the argument of the preceding chapters a step farther – or, more precisely, to make explicit one of its

---

[1] *Discours sur la permission de liberté de religion, dicte Religions-Vrede au Pays-Bais* (1559), quoted from E. H. Kossman and A. F. Mellink, trans. and eds., *Texts Concerning the Revolt of the Netherlands* (Cambridge University Press, 1974), p. 163.

implications. Just now I said that it was the fact that northwest Europe found it impossible to recover religious unity, after it had been fractured by Protestantism, that made it thoroughly implausible to think any longer in terms of the "two rules" doctrine. The "two rules" doctrine assumes that, within a given political jurisdiction, membership in the church is coterminous with citizenship in the polity, small and marginalized groups such as the Jews being an exception. What eventually emerged from this rethinking, I observed in the preceding chapter, was our rights-limited states. This rethinking followed many paths. But what I want now to argue is something hinted at in the preceding chapters but not developed, namely, that when we put what Paul says in Romans about the task and authority of the state together with the political implications of the nature and existence of the church, what we get is an argument for a state that is limited in exactly the sort of way that our liberal democracies are limited.

Calvin's understanding of the task of government – to encourage and coerce good behavior – is an example of what in recent years has come to be called a "perfectionist" understanding. In concluding my discussion of his view I observed that the perfectionist understanding of the state carries with it no implications concerning limits on the state's authority; it is entirely consistent with the perfectionist understanding for the state to forbid the people to assemble on the ground that assembling would encourage bad behavior. The claim that it would encourage bad behavior might be mistaken; but it's not inconsistent with the perfectionist understanding to forbid public assemblies for that reason. The perfectionist theorist might argue for *adding* some principle of limits on state authority; but the perfectionist understanding itself does not imply any limits. And as we saw, Calvin held that there are no limits on the authority of government, other than those imposed by the jurisdiction of the church and by the fact that any directive the state may issue that requires violating the First Table of the Decalogue is without authority.

Contrast that with Paul's description of what God authorizes the state to do. Paul does not say that God authorizes the state to pressure citizens into what it regards as pious and virtuous behavior; he says that God authorizes the state to curb and punish wrongdoing. I argued that this implies that the state must not itself wrong either the citizens individually or their institutions, whether in the course of trying to curb the citizens' wronging of each other or in the course of some other project of the state. It must honor their natural rights.[2] That there are normative, rights-based, limits on state authority is implicit in what Paul says God authorizes government to do.

In principle the constitution or fundamental law of a rights-limited state might impose normative limits on the authority of the state that look very different from those that we are familiar with in our present-day liberal democratic states; that would be the case if the authors of the constitution or fundamental law had very different views as to the natural rights of citizens and their institutions from those we have. So now let's add to the picture the conclusions we arrived at concerning the political implications of the nature and existence of the church. If the church is to "be itself," it must have institutional autonomy from the state; and both those citizens who are members of the church and those who are not must enjoy religious freedom. That freedom includes, but goes well beyond, the civil right of members of the church to the "free exercise" of their religion.

---

[2] In *Justice: Rights and Wrongs* (Princeton University Press, 2008) I develop a theory of natural rights.

Christians will of course hold that God *authorizes* the church to be itself, thereby also forbidding the state to do anything that infringes on the institutional autonomy of the church or the religious freedom of the citizens. These are normative limits on the state's authority with respect to religion. Paul's teaching concerning what it is that God authorizes government to do, when combined with implications drawn from the existence and nature of the church, implies that wherever the church is present in society, the state is normatively limited with respect to religion. The last step in the argument is that these normative limits on the authority of the state with respect to religion are almost exactly the same as those imposed on the American state by its constitution and fundamental law. And the United States is, of course, an example of a rights-limited democracy – commonly called a *liberal* democracy.

The rights-limited democracies that we are familiar with are normatively limited in other ways as well; the freedom from state interference definitive of such polities goes well beyond freedom with respect to religion. But there can be little doubt that, historically, the struggle for freedom with respect to religion was at the heart of the transition from Christendom to our rights-limited democracies, and that once this freedom was granted, a number of others seemed well-nigh inevitable. If one allows citizens to present their religious convictions freely to others, why would one not allow them to speak freely about most other matters as well?

Some readers will be feeling uneasy at this point in the argument. Is it not altogether implausible to suppose that Paul's brief remarks in his letter to the Christians in Rome, coupled with the political implication of the existence and nature of the church, would vindicate the fundamental structure of governments of the modern West, namely, liberal democracy? Can we take seriously the claim of serendipity lurking here, especially since Paul has seldom before been interpreted as propounding a rights-protecting and rights-honoring understanding of government and since the long tradition of "two rules" thinking never interpreted the existence and nature of the church as having the implications that I have claimed they have?

I understand the uneasiness. Implicit in my argument is indeed an assumption of serendipity. But uneasiness over the serendipity is not an answer to the line of argument that I have developed.

I anticipate another objection as well, this to the effect that the serendipity is only apparent. Liberal democracies, as we know them in the West today, have an "idea" behind them, an implicit commitment to values or principles that make sense of the whole; they are not just fortuitous collocations of disparate elements. I have tacitly been assuming that a central component in the governing idea of these polities is that the natural rights of citizens place normative limits on the authority of government. But I am mistaken about this, says the objector. That is not the governing idea. It is no accident that these are commonly called *liberal* democracies. The governing idea is that everybody is to be *free* to form and enact his or her own plan of life. What shapes these polities is the assumption that personal autonomy is the supreme political good. In our world of conflicting life-plans this core idea must, of course, be qualified; there could not possibly be a polity that assures everybody equal autonomy. One of the most common suggestions as to the qualification is this: everybody is to have as much freedom as is compatible with the same freedom for others – call it *maximal compatible* freedom.

But, so the objector continues, a Christian cannot accept autonomy as the supreme political good. The governing idea of a liberal polity is antithetical to Christian conviction. Christians should be thankful for many of the freedoms allowed by a liberal polity. But only if one were completely oblivious to the governing idea of the liberal polity would the thought cross one's mind that Paul's teaching concerning the task and authority of government, coupled with the political implications of the nature and existence of the church, implies that the state should be what we know as the liberal democratic state.

My response is twofold. First, it is by no means obvious that Christians should be opposed to a polity whose governing idea is that everybody is to enjoy maximal compatible freedom. Of course Christians do not believe that it is morally acceptable for everybody to do whatever he or she wishes. But compatibility is a significant constraint on freedom. And as we have seen several times over, from the fact that it is morally wrong to do something it does not follow that citizens should be legally proscribed from doing it. Life would be a horror if every form of wrongdoing were illegal; there would not be enough police to go around.

But second, I hold that this analysis of liberal democracy is mistaken; maximal compatible freedom is not the governing idea. I have argued this point elsewhere and at length; any rehearsal of the argument that I could give here would have to be too brief and cryptic to be of any use.[3] I hold that the governing idea of liberal democracy is not maximal compatible freedom but the right to equal political voice of all adult citizens, the exercise of this voice to be conducted within the framework of a constitution that

---

[3] The argument is to be found in Part 1 and Part 2 of my *Understanding Liberal Democracy*, ed. Terence Cuneo (Oxford University Press, forthcoming).

protects citizens from the passage of laws that require or permit the state to violate their fundamental natural rights, one of those natural rights being the right to equal political voice.

As I have noted several times, Paul's picture of the state as a rights-protecting and rights-limited institution is no more than a framework; it does not tell us which are the rights that the state must honor. Our drawing-out the political implications of the nature and existence of the church filled in the framework with respect to the religious rights of citizens and their institutions. The emergence in the seventeenth and eighteenth centuries of the idea that citizens have an equal right to political voice within a constitutional framework filled in another part of the framework.

I mentioned in Chapter 11 that a complaint against the rights-limited state commonly heard nowadays, coming from traditionalists and conservatives, Christian and non-Christian alike, is that since the citizens of such states no longer share a religious and moral ethos to which the state can appeal, the liberal democratic state is an amoral *modus vivendi*, inherently unstable, bound to degenerate into a bureaucratic and technocratic horror.

But this is just mistaken. From the fact that the modern liberal democratic state cannot be the political expression of the shared religious and moral ethos of the people, since there is no such shared ethos to express, it does not follow that it is an amoral arrangement of convenience. The liberal democratic state is like every other state in having a moral task that it was authorized by God to perform, the task of curbing injustice. This implies that it cannot be morally neutral; how could it be? Its issuing of legislation presupposes moral conviction; the legislation it issues instructs the citizens in the ways of justice and injustice. And to say it yet one more time, there are normative limits on its authority. It must not violate the natural rights of the citizens; it must not itself perpetrate injustice. The rights-protecting and rights-limited state is inherently a moral enterprise.

But are its citizens in fact alert to injustice? Are they capable of recognizing injustice when it occurs? Are they disposed to struggle against it when they recognize it? It is on these points that worries about the stability and endurance of the rights-protecting and rights-limited state should be focused. By virtue of how God's governance of humankind is effectuated, human beings who have emerged from infancy have some sense of justice. But that sense of justice is distorted and inhibited by greed, by the "isms" and ideologies to which we fall prey, by stories we tell about "the other," by the dismay and fear we feel at the prospect of what would have to change if we acknowledged that we were wronging the other. If the rights-protecting and rights-limited state does not endure, it will be because of those distortions and inhibitions, not because it is an amoral enterprise.

CHAPTER 14

Institutional rights as limits on the authority of the state

In our opening chapters I noted that society is pervaded by the phenomenon of social entities with authority structures, including governance-authority structures. In those chapters I said nothing about the relation of such entities to each other. But from our discussion of the political implications of the nature and existence of the church there emerged a point, concerning that relation, whose importance cannot be overemphasized. The authority of the church places normative limits on the authority of the state. If the church has the authority to do certain things, then the state does not have the right to prevent it from doing those things. Should the state try to prevent the church from doing those things, it exceeds its authority.

It will be obvious that this is not a peculiarity of the relation of the church to the state but one instance of a general principle: if institution A has the authority to perform action x, then institution B does not have the right to prevent A from doing x. There is one sort of exception to the principle. In certain contest situations, an individual or institution may have the authority (permission-right) to do x while another individual or institution has the right to try to prevent him or it from doing x. In such situations, having the permission-right to do x does not carry along with it the claim-right to being free to do x. Usually, however, these two rights, the permission-right to do x and the claim-right to being free to do x, come together; when they do, the principle cited holds.

Consider the following situation: person A has the authority to do x by virtue of person B having authorized A to do x; but in authorizing A to do x, B stipulated that he reserved the right to withdraw that authorization at any time. Now suppose that A tries to do x and B tries to prevent A from doing x; would this not be an exception to the principle? Doesn't B have the authority to try to prevent A from doing x should he so desire? No, not unless B has withdrawn his authorization, in which case A is not authorized to do x. This is not an exception to the principle.

Those who write about normative limits on the liberal democratic state almost always have in mind the rights of individuals against the state as the source of those limits. Citizens have a natural right against the state to be free to speak in public; that's the ground of the normative limit on the state's authority to curb the speech of its citizens. But as we have just now seen, there are also normative limits placed on the authority of the state by the presence in society of a wide range of social entities with authority structures, these including the church, business enterprises, educational institutions, and so forth. The authority of our imaginary furniture-making enterprise to do what it does places limits on the authority of the state.

It is not only when thinking about the normative limits on the state's authority that we must keep in mind the wide range of other authority structures to be found in society; we must also keep that panoply in mind when reflecting on the *task* of the state. Government is by no means the only social entity with an authority structure that wrongs individuals. It is true of such entities in general that they can and do wrong people. They can and do wrong each other. And individuals can and do wrong them. If the state is to carry out its task of curbing wrongdoing, it cannot attend only to the actions of individuals but must attend to the actions of social entities as well.

A theorist who reflected extensively on the authority and task of the state with the full range in mind of social entities with authority structures, and who did so within a Christian theological framework, was the Dutch theologian and statesman Abraham Kuyper. Kuyper's writings on the matter have proved enormously influential. So rather than speaking in my own voice I will here speak in Kuyper's voice – this in spite of the fact that his voice is rather often too flamboyant and Romantic for my taste.

In the last quarter of the twentieth century there was a great deal of discussion about so-called *mediating structures*, the idea behind calling them "mediating structures" being that they mediate between the state and individuals.[1] Both Kuyper and the mediating-structures theorists argue that the presence and vitality of social entities independent of the state are indispensable to the health of society; their vigor puts a brake on the expansionist tendencies of the state. What is nearly missing in the mediating-structures theorists, however, is the very thing that is prominent in Kuyper's discussion, namely, a discussion of the rights of such entities and of the way in which their rights place limits on the authority of the state. It is this feature of Kuyper's discussion that makes it relevant to our purposes here. There are rather clear adumbrations of Kuyper's ideas on this matter in Althusius.[2] What Kuyper added is an idea that we will be getting to shortly, namely, that of *spheres*.

[1] For a theological approach to the topic, see Michael Novak, *Democracy and Mediating Strucures: A Theological Inquiry* (Washington, DC: American Enterprise Institute, 1980).
[2] For an excellent discussion of Althusius, see chapter 3 of John Witte's *The Reformation of Rights: Law, Religion, and Human Rights in Early Modern Calvinism* (Cambridge University Press, 2007).

Kuyper more or less took for granted that the jurisdiction of one authority structure places limits on the jurisdiction of all other authority structures; he did not articulate and argue the point. What he instead spent time arguing in the Stone Lectures is that in a well-ordered and well-functioning society, there will be a multiplicity of authority structures whose authority is non-derived – that is, a multiplicity of authority structures whose authority has not been conferred on those structures by some other authority structure, in particular, not by the state. Let's see how he develops the point.

When regarded in its totality, the story of humankind on earth is not the story of the same old things happening over and over but a story of progress. This story of progress is the story of the progressive actualization by human beings of "the powers which, by virtue of the ordinances of creation, are innate in nature itself." Theoretical learning is "the application to the cosmos of the powers of investigation and thought created within us." Art is "the natural productivity of our imagination."[3] And so forth. The picture Kuyper draws is that of human existence, seen in its totality, as teeming with creative vitality. This development does not take place by each individual doing his own thing; in good measure it takes place, and can only take place, by individuals working together to achieve shared goals. Kuyper typically employs organic metaphors to make the point. The "expressions of life" in theoretical learning, art, business, and so forth, "all together . . . form the life of creation, in accord with the ordinances of creation, and therefore are *organically* developed" (118). "The development is spontaneous, just as that of the stem and the branches of a plant" (117).

---

[3] Abraham Kuyper, *Calvinism: The Stone Lectures for 1898–1899* (New York: Fleming H. Revell Co., n.d.), p. 118. References are henceforth incorporated into the text.

In order to work together to achieve our shared goals we find it useful, and often necessary, to establish organizations and institutions. Scholarship could not flourish without an institutional base in such organizations as universities, research institutes, and publishing houses; the arts could not flourish without an institutional base in such organizations as conservatories, galleries, and opera houses; recreation could not flourish without such organizations as chess clubs and baseball teams.

Each of such social entities has the authority to do certain things, that is, the right and power (*potestas*) to do them, among the things they have the authority to do being the authority to issue directives on certain matters to certain people. Kuyper usually calls this sort of institutional authority "sovereignty"; on occasion he calls it "dominion" or "power." "The University exercises scientific dominion; the Academy of fine arts is possessed of art-power; the guild exercised a technical dominion; the trades-union rules over labor ... Behind these organic spheres, with intellectual, aesthetical and technical sovereignty, the sphere of the family opens itself, with its rights of marriage, domestic peace, education and possession" (123).

Kuyper is emphatic that we have a natural right to form institutional authority structures; it is not a purely positive right that we possess on account of the state or some other institution having delegated it to us. The state is authorized to regulate this natural right for the purpose of securing justice and the common good; and some social entities, such as limited liability corporations, are creatures of the law. But we have a natural right to get together to establish a college, a musical organization, a chess club. "The family, the business, science, art, and so forth are all social [institutions], which do not owe their existence to the state, and which do not derive the law of their life from the superiority of the state, but obey a higher authority within their own bosom" (116).

Kuyper's repeated and emphatic insistence on our natural right to get together to establish social entities with authority structures, without asking permission of the state, can seem to you and me like hyperventilating. We, those of us who are present-day Americans, get together to establish institutions and organizations all the time without asking permission of the state. But Kuyper was writing with the memory still fresh of the French Revolution and its attempt to get the bulk of organizations under the control of the state. On June 14, 1791, the National Assembly passed a law whose first article reads, "Since the abolition of all kinds of corporations of citizens of the same occupation and profession is one of the fundamental principles of the French Constitution, re-establishment thereof under any pretext or form whatsoever is forbidden." The content of this article found its way, in one form and another, into the constitution.[4]

If we have a natural right to establish social entities with authority structures to serve our common good, the state perforce does not have a right to forbid us to do so. "Neither the life of science nor of art, nor of agriculture, nor of industry, nor of commerce, nor of navigation, nor of the family, nor of human relationship may be coerced to suit itself to the grace of the government. The State may never become an octopus, which stifles the whole of life" (124). That which an institution has the authority to do, the state is not permitted to prevent it from doing. Institutions with authority structures have moral rights against the state. To this Kuyper adds, "As you feel at once, this is the deeply interesting question of our civil liberties" (116).

---

[4] I owe this information to Dale van Kley.

Kuyper's thought on these matters has often been compared to the doctrine, prominent in modern Catholic social thought, of *subsidiarity*. I will have to leave it to others to trace out the similarities and differences.[5]

If the teeming multitude of authority structures in civil society do not get their authority by authorization from the state, from where do they get their authority? Kuyper's answer is that "the rights and liberties of social life [come] from the same source from which the high authority of the government flows – even the *absolute sovereignty of God*. From this *one* source in God, *sovereignty in the individual sphere*, in the family and in every social circle, is just as directly derived as the *supremacy of State authority*" (126–27). In all cases, the "inherent authority is sovereign, that is to say, it has above itself nothing but God" (121). Authority in all its forms is divinely delegated authority. God, our "supreme Sovereign," "delegates his authority to human beings, so that on earth one never

---

[5] There are, in my judgment, two fundamental differences. The term "subsidiarity" unmistakably suggests a hierarchical picture of society. Kuyper would reject this picture. He would insist that a university, for example, is not subsidiary to anything whatsoever. Second, the classic defense of subsidiarity, in the papal encyclical *Quadragesimo anno*, is thoroughly consequentialist; subsidiarity makes for a better society and a better state. Kuyper's approach is a rights-based approach: we have a natural right to form authority structures and the state must respect the right of these structures to exercise their authority. In discussions by Catholics of subsidiarity one sometimes finds both of these points of contrast, especially the former, softened in Kuyper's direction. Rather often they reject the hierarchical picture suggested by the term "subsidiarity," and they sometimes speak about the non-derived right of, say, universities to exercise authority and the limits that this places on the authority of the state. My own sense, concerning the latter point, is that Catholic writers have not fully integrated their basic consequentialist defense with a rights-based defense. Two helpful essays on these matters are Russell Hittinger, "Social Pluralism and Subsidiarity in Catholic Social Doctrine," and Kenneth Grasso, "The Subsidiary State: Society, the State, and the Principle of Subsidiarity in Catholic Social Thought," both in Jeanne Heffernan Schindler, ed., *Christianity and Civil Society* (Lanham, MD: Lexington Books, 2008), pp. 11–29, 33–65.

directly encounters God Himself in visible things but always sees his sovereign authority exercised in *human* office."[6]

Kuyper was fierce in his insistence that no human being or institution just comes with the right to issue binding directives to another. All authority to issue binding directives to human beings is grounded in God's authorizing of persons and institutions to do so. What Kuyper says in the context of his discussion of governmental authority is clearly meant to apply to authority in general.

> Authority over men cannot arise from men ... When God says to me, "obey," then I humbly bow my head, without compromising in the least my personal dignity as a man. For in like proportion as you degrade yourself, by bowing low to a child of man, whose breath is in his nostrils, so, on the other hand, do you raise yourself, if you submit to the authority of the Lord of heaven and earth. (104)

I do not see how these claims of Kuyper, about the source of institutional authority, can be correct in the general form in which Kuyper makes them. Suppose that a group of us get together to form a chess club. We compose some bylaws spelling out a governance structure for our projected organization, we do whatever is necessary to get the organization up and running, and shortly the club issues directives to its membership. Institutional authority has emerged from the actions of our group, this authority being in many cases *binding* authority. Institutions that hire employees in order to make products for the public or to offer

---

[6] Abraham Kuyper, "Sphere Sovereignty," in James Bratt, ed., *Abraham Kuyper: A Centennial Reader* (Grand Rapids: Wm. B. Eerdmans Publishing Co., 1998), p. 466. Cf. Kuyper, *Calvinism*, p. 108: "No one on earth can claim authority over his fellowmen, unless it be laid upon him '*by the grace of God*'; and therefore, the ultimate duty of obedience, is imposed upon us not by man, but by God himself." And ibid., 106: "God only – and never any creature – is possessed of sovereign rights, in the destiny of nations, because God alone created them, maintains them by His Almighty power, and rules them, by his ordinances ... Man never possesses power over his fellow-man, in any other way than by an authority which descends upon him from the majesty of God."

services are somewhat different from membership organizations; but in their case, too, authority emerges from human action. "Authority over men cannot arise from men," says Kuyper. This is not true in general. The fact that it is not true in general makes no difference to Kuyper's overall line of argument, however.

In a well-functioning modern society there will be a multiplicity of institutions and organizations with authority structures. The state is one of these, one among many. It is a very distinctive one-among-many, however. To highlight a fundamental aspect of what makes it distinctive Kuyper sometimes called the authority of the state *mechanical* as distinct from *organic*. "The sovereignty of God, in its descent upon men, separates itself into two spheres. On the one hand the mechanical sphere of *State-authority*, and on the other hand the organic sphere of the authority of the *Social circles*. [In both spheres] the inherent authority is sovereign, that is to say, it has above itself nothing but God" (121).

What did Kuyper mean by calling the authority of the state "mechanical"? The actualization of humankind's in-created potentials gives rise not only to institutional bases for scholarship, the arts, economic activity, and the like, along with their authority structures, but also to states. The "impulse to form states arises from man's social nature," says Kuyper, adding that this thought "was expressed already by Aristotle when he called man a [political animal]" (100). In that respect the state is as much an organic development as are universities, art academies, and the like. But in this fallen world of ours the dominant task of the state has become to restrain wrongdoing and secure justice. As such, the state is a primary instrument of what Kuyper called God's *common grace*. Kuyper speculates that had there been no wrongdoing, political life "would have evolved itself, after a patriarchal fashion, from the life of the family" (101). There would have been no magistrates, no police, no army. In fact, however, every state is a "means of compelling order and of guaranteeing a safe course of life." As such it is "mechanical," "always something unnatural," "something against which the deeper aspirations of our nature rebel" (ibid.). "*God has instituted the magistrates, by reason of sin*"; they "rule mechanically, and do not harmonize with our nature" (102).

Not only is the magistrates' relation to human development "mechanical" in this way, rather than "organic"; the magistrates are themselves fallen. In one direction, they give in to the temptation to expand the authority of the state beyond its proper scope; in the other direction, they give in to the temptation to allow the authority of the state to be unduly restricted. Hence there is always a duality in the Christian attitude toward the state. We "gratefully . . . receive, from the hand of God, the institution of the State with its magistrates, as a means of preservation, now indeed indispensable." But we must also "ever watch against the danger, which lurks, for our personal liberty, in the power of the State" (102–03) as well as in its ineffectiveness.

This, so far, is negative. The state "must occupy its own place, on its own root, among all the other trees of the forest, and thus it has to honour and maintain every form of life, which grows independently, in its own sacred autonomy" (124). What is the positive task of the state?

Strictly speaking, there is no distinct type of social activity over which the state is sovereign; in that way, too, it is unlike other authority structures. The state is, as it were, "the *sphere of spheres*, which encircles the whole extent of human life."[7] So what then is its task? Its task is threefold: "1. Whenever different spheres [authority structures] clash, to compel mutual regard for the

---

[7] Kuyper, "Sphere Sovereignty," p. 472.

boundary-lines of each; 2. To defend individuals and the weak ones, in those spheres [authority structures], against the abuse of power of the rest; and 3. To coerce all together to bear *personal* and *financial* burdens for the maintenance of the natural unity of the State" (124–25).

And what is the overarching goal of the state in its interventions? Justice and certain aspects of the common good. "The highest duty of the government remains therefore unchangeably that of *justice*, and in the second place it has to care for the people as a unity, partly *at home*, in order that its unity may grow ever deeper and may not be disturbed, and partly *abroad*, lest the national existence suffer harm" (130).

So far and no farther. "A people ... which abandons to State Supremacy the right of the family, or a University, which abandons to it the right of science, is just as guilty before God, as a nation which lays its hands upon the rights of the magistrates. And thus the struggle for liberty is not only declared permissible, but is made a duty for each individual in his own sphere" (127). The best protection against state aggrandizement is a vital civil society and a vigorous defense thereof. Something has gone profoundly wrong in society when few institutions have the legal authority to do anything without being authorized by the state. The state has then become a menace.

Kuyper became famous for the slogan that originated as the title of his rectoral address at the founding of the Free University of Amsterdam in 1880, "Souvereiniteit in eigen kring." The slogan translates literally into somewhat awkward English as "Sovereignty in its own sphere." More simply: "Sphere sovereignty." What did Kuyper have in mind by the slogan? Though he himself always discussed together the two

ideas of *sovereignty* and *sphere*, they are clearly distinct, the
former being more fundamental than the latter.[8]

What we have seen so far is that in a well-ordered society there
will be a large number of distinct authority structures with limited
jurisdiction and non-derived authority; where that is not the case
we can be sure, Kuyper argued, that social progress is being
stymied or injustice perpetrated. That leaves open the question
of how these distinct jurisdictions in a well-ordered society are to
be determined. It was in his answer to this question that Kuyper
employed the idea of a sphere. In a well-ordered society, no
institutional authority structure will have a jurisdiction that
extends into more than one sphere, nor will any institution try
to exert influence on the institutions in another sphere.[9]

What is a *sphere?* Kuyper never offered an explanation.
He assumed that his readers already had a sufficiently firm
grip on the concept for him to be able to employ it without
explanation. And indeed, to this day the social discourse of all
of us is full of references to what Kuyper called *spheres*. Kuyper
would have called each of the following "a sphere": business,
politics, education, the arts, recreation, medicine, law, religion,
banking, manufacturing, and service industries. We speak of
"the world of the arts," we speak of "the banking sector," and
so forth. What we mean by "world" and "sector" is what

---

[8] I have yet to come across any account of Kuyper's thought in which the two ideas are
clearly distinguished and discussed separately; this holds also for my own previous
expositions of Kuyper's thought.

[9] The title of Michael Walzer's book *Spheres of Justice: A Defense of Pluralism and Equality*
(New York: Basic Books, 1983) might suggest that his topic is the same as Kuyper's. It is
not. His idea of spheres is roughly the same as Kuyper's; and Kuyper would agree with
Walzer's fundamental thesis, that there are different types of goods in different spheres.
But the topic of Walzer's book is the just distribution of those different types of goods in
different spheres. As we shall see, that is not Kuyper's concern. His concern is authority
and infringements on authority. The word "authority" does not make it into the index of
Walzer's book.

Kuyper meant by a "sphere."[10] The idea was in the air in Kuyper's time; it remains in the air today.

Max Weber famously employed the idea of a sphere (sector, domain, world) in his account of modernization. At the heart of modernization, so Weber claimed, was the "differentiation" of human activity into distinct spheres, life within each of these distinct spheres being shaped and formed by the pursuit of a distinct good. But whereas for the most part Weber employed the idea descriptively, Kuyper employed the idea normatively.[11] Sharing with Weber the view that modernization has resulted in the differentiation of human activity into a number of distinct spheres, Kuyper went on to argue that in a well-ordered modernized society, no institution would have jurisdiction within more than one sphere, nor would any institution intrude itself into the workings of institutions outside its own sphere. The full picture of a multiplicity of entities with authority structures, the jurisdiction of each being confined to its own sphere, is compellingly summarized in the following lengthy but vivid passage from Kuyper's rectoral address of 1880:

The cogwheels of all these spheres engage each other, and precisely through that interaction emerges the rich, multifaceted multiformity of human life. Hence also rises the danger that one sphere in life may encroach on its neighbor like a sticky wheel that shears off one cog after

[10] I must add that in the examples he gives of spheres, Kuyper sometimes seems to me to be confusing things. For example, he speaks in one place of "the social life of cities and villages [as forming] a sphere of existence" distinct from that of the country as a whole. "Sphere" is here used to refer to something quite different from a domain, a sector, a "world." See Kuyper, *Calvinism*, p. 123.

[11] In two lectures that he gave late in his life, "Politics as a Vocation" and "Science as a Vocation," Weber employed the idea normatively in exactly the same way that Kuyper did. The lectures can be found in H. H. Gerth and C. Wright Mills, trans. and eds., *From Max Weber: Essays in Sociology* (New York: Oxford University Press, 1946), pp. 77–156.

another until the whole operation is disrupted. Hence also the raison d'etre for the special sphere of authority that emerged in the State. It must provide for sound mutual interaction among the various spheres, insofar as they are externally manifest, and keep them within just limits. Furthermore, since personal life can be suppressed by the group in which one lives, the state must protect the individual from the tyranny of his own circle. This Sovereign, as Scripture tersely puts it, "gives stability to the land by justice" (Prov. 26:4), for *without* justice it destroys itself and falls. Thus the sovereignty of the State, as the power that protects the individual and defines the mutual relationships among the visible spheres, rises high *above* them by its right to command and compel. But *within* these spheres that does not obtain. There another authority rules, an authority that descends directly from God apart from the State. This authority the State does not *confer* but *acknowledge*. Even in defining laws for the mutual relationships among the spheres, the State may not set its own will as the standard but is *bound* by the choice of a Higher will, as expressed in the nature and purpose of these spheres. The State must see that the wheels operate as intended. Not to suppress life nor to shackle freedom but to make possible the free movement of life in and for every sphere: does not this ideal beckon every nobler head of state?[12]

Not only do we continue to employ the concept of a sphere; we continue to employ the concept in the same normative way that Kuyper employed it. Kuyper's oft-repeated concern about the aggrandizing tendencies of the church have lost their relevance, being replaced in spades by concerns about the aggrandizing tendencies of the state and of business. And over and over one hears these aggrandizing tendencies of state and business described in terms of the institutions of one sphere interfering in the affairs of those in another sphere. Business is charged with having undue influence on politics, on education, on news, on art; the state is charged with having undue influence on business, on banking, on agriculture; and so forth. This is Kuyperian thinking.

[12] "Sphere Sovereignty," pp. 467–68.

But institutional aggrandizement does not only take the form of an institution trying to act or exert influence in some sphere other than its own; it also takes the form of an institution becoming monopolistic within its own sphere. Banks become "too big to fail." Curiously, Kuyper took no note of such intra-sector institutional aggrandizement.

As I mentioned earlier, those who write about normative limits on the liberal democratic state almost always have in mind the rights of individuals against the state as the source of those limits. Citizens have a natural right against the state to be free to speak in public; that's the ground of the normative limit on the state's authority to curb the speech of its citizens. What we have seen in Kuyper is a fascinatingly different approach, not incompatible but different, an institutionalist rather than individualist approach. Kuyper affirmed that individual citizens have rights against the state. But what he emphasized was the normative limits placed on the authority of the state by the presence in society of a wide range of social entities with authority structures. We have a natural right to get together to establish such social entities as may serve our common purposes without asking leave of the state to do so; the authority inherent within the entities that we establish then places limits on the authority of the state.

CHAPTER 15

Wrap-up: Polycarp re-visited

In Polycarp's predicament, there in the stadium in Smyrna on February 22, 156, we discerned two dualities and several ironies. As a citizen of Smyrna, Polycarp was under the authority of Caesar and his proconsul; as a bishop of the church, he himself exercised authority in the name of Christ. Two authority structures intersecting in Polycarp. The proconsul was now ordering Polycarp to renounce the one in whose name he, Polycarp, exercised authority in the church, namely, Christ. The authority structures intersecting in Polycarp were in collision with each other.

In the authority of Caesar and his proconsul there was another duality. Caesar and his proconsul were among the "princes and authorities appointed by God"; in their exercise of authority they mediated God's authority. In ordering Polycarp to renounce Christ the proconsul was now ordering Polycarp to renounce the one who had appointed him, the proconsul, and Caesar, namely, God. For in a way that had not yet been articulated, Christ was God.

Polycarp's view, that at least some political authorities have been appointed by God, had apparently become a commonplace among Christians. He says that "we [Christians] have been taught to render honour, as is meet, if it hurts us not, to princes and authorities appointed by God." The language echoes that of Paul in Romans 13.

Let us agree that it was morally wrong for the proconsul to order Polycarp to renounce Christ his king. Given that it was morally wrong, our reflections led us to the conclusion that the proconsul lacked the moral authority to issue his order. No doubt the position of authority that the proconsul occupied gave him the *legal* authority to order Polycarp to renounce Christ; he had what I called the *positional authority* to issue his order. But that did not give him the moral authority to do so. And since he lacked the moral authority to issue his order, his order did not generate in Polycarp an obligation to obey, not even a *prima facie* obligation. Polycarp was not in the predicament of having a conflict of *prima facie* obligations.

Our reflections also led to the conclusion that the proconsul's order exceeded what God has authorized (appointed) government to do. God has authorized government to serve his providential purposes by curbing wrongdoing. Rather than curbing wrongdoing, the proconsul's directive was itself a case of wrongdoing.

There was no confusion in Polycarp's mind between the church in Smyrna and the mob in the stadium, nor, more generally, between church and empire. Though he and his fellow Christians in the area were both members of the church and subjects of the empire, it was obvious to all of them that the church was a distinct people from the subjects of the empire. When Europe became Christianized, this sense of distinctness fell away and the idea emerged that the citizenry of a state was more or less coterminous with the membership of the church in that area; the difference between church and state was then understood as a difference in jurisdiction. Today it is once again obvious that the membership of the church in a certain area is not coterminous with the citizenry of the state that has jurisdiction in that area.

Understanding the church along the lines implicit in Polycarp's declarations, I drew out the political implications of the nature and existence of the church and noted how similar those implications are to the constitutional and legal guarantees for religious institutions and practice in liberal democracies. In no liberal democracy would it be constitutionally or legally permissible for an official to do what Stadius Quadratus ordered Polycarp to do, namely, renounce Christ.

Does this mean that no citizen of a liberal democracy will find himself or herself in Polycarp's predicament? Have we in the modern West finally succeeded in putting behind us the possibility of a Polycarp? We have not. We must expect that there will be ever new episodes of citizens finding that their religious convictions collide with what the state, acting within its legal and constitutional limits, orders them to do or refrain from doing. The ongoing controversy in France over the attempt of the state to specify when and where Muslim women may be veiled is just one example of the point.

Why is this? Why must we continue to expect episodes of confrontation? For two reasons, one from the side of religion and one from the side of the state.

From the side of religion, though some forms of religion confine themselves to the private sphere, there have always been religions that refused to do so; we can say with confidence that there always will be. For Islam, how Muslim women appear in public carries religious import.

From the side of the state, the civil right to freedom of religious practice and the civil right of religious institutions to autonomy vis-à-vis the state are *prima facie* civil rights, not absolute, *ultima facie*, rights. Over and over again the state finds itself forced to decide whether, in a given case, the civil right to religious freedom is outweighed by the civil right to some other social good. The widespread de-churching of Western Europe has led the European

Union and various of its member states regularly to rank the right to equal treatment of one sort or another higher than the right to freedom of religion. Thus it is that the British High Court recently declared that the Derby City Council had the authority to deny the request of a couple, Eunice and Owen Johns, to foster a child, the ground of the denial being that the couple's conservative Christian convictions might lead them to transmit to the child negative attitudes concerning homosexuality.[1] In the United States, the erosion of religious freedom is more likely to come about by the courts treating religious rights as a special case of the right to free speech and then imposing on the practice of religion whatever restrictions are deemed appropriate for speech.

Only if liberal democracies are subverted into something else will we see martyrdoms. But we must expect that collisions of authority, similar to that which took place on that fateful day in the stadium in Smyrna, will continue.

---

[1] The full title of the case is this: *R. (on the application of Johns and Johns) v. Derby City Council; Equality and Human Rights Commission (intervening)* [2011] EWHC 375 (admin).

Bibliography

Aquinas, T., *St Thomas Aquinas: Political Writings*, trans. and ed. R. W. Dyson (Cambridge University Press, 2002).

Aristotle, *Complete Works*, ed. J. Barnes (Princeton University Press, 1984).

Augustine, *The City of God against the Pagans*, trans. and ed. R. W. Dyson (Cambridge University Press, 1998).

Barth, K., *Community, State, and Church* (Garden City, NY: Anchor Books, Doubleday & Co., 1960).

Berkhof, H., *Christ and the Powers*, trans. J. H. Yoder (Scottdale, PA: Herald Press, 1962).

Berryman, J., *Love & Fame* (New York: Farrar, Straus, and Giroux, 1970).

Bratt, J., trans. and ed., *Abraham Kuyper: A Centennial Reader* (Grand Rapids: Wm. B. Eerdmans Publishing Co., 1998).

Calvin, J., *Institutes of the Christian Religion*, trans. F. L. Battles (Philadelphia: Westminster Press, 1950).

Chernaik, W., "Biblical Republicanism," *Prose Studies*, 23:1 (April 2000), 147–60.

Ehler, S. Z., *Twenty Centuries of Church and State: A Survey of their Relations in Past and Present* (Westminster, MD: Newman Press, 1957).

Ehler, S. Z., and J. B. Morrall, trans. and eds., *Church and State through the Centuries: A Collection of Historic Documents with Commentaries* (New York: Biblo and Tannen, 1967).

Eisenbaum, P., *Paul Was Not a Christian: The Original Message of a Misunderstood Apostle* (New York: HarperOne, 2009).

Flannery, A., OP, ed., *Vatican Council II: The Conciliar and Post Conciliar Documents* (Northport, NY: Costello Publishing Co., 1975).

Friedman, R. B., "On the Concept of Authority in Political Philosophy," in R. E. Flathman, ed., *Concepts in Social & Political Philosophy* (New York: Macmillan Publishing Co., 1973), pp. 121–46.

Gerth, H. H., and C. W. Mills, trans. and eds., *From Max Weber: Essays in Sociology* (Oxford University Press, 1946).

Gilbert, M., *A Theory of Political Obligation* (Oxford: Clarendon Press, 2006).

Goppelt, L., *A Commentary on I Peter* (Grand Rapids: Wm. B. Eerdmans Publishing Co., 1993).

Gordon, B., *Calvin* (New Haven: Yale University Press, 2009).

Grasso, K., "The Subsidiary State: Society, the State, and the Principle of Subsidiarity in Catholic Social Thought," in J. H. Schindler, ed., *Christianity and Civil Society* (Lanham, MD: Lexington Books, 2008), pp. 33–65.

Green, L., *The Authority of the State* (Oxford: Clarendon Press, 1988).

Hauerwas, S., and W. H. Willimon, *Resident Aliens* (Nashville: Abingdon Press, 1989).

Hittinger, R., "Social Pluralism and Subsidiarity in Catholic Social Doctrine," in J. H. Schindler, ed., *Christianity and Civil Society* (Lanham, MD: Lexington Books, 2008), pp. 11–29.

Klosko, G., *Political Obligations* (Oxford University Press, 2005).

Kossman E. H., and A. F. Mellink, trans. and eds., *Texts Concerning the Revolt of the Netherlands* (Cambridge University Press, 1974).

Kuyper, A., *Calvinism: The Stone Lectures for 1898–1899* (New York: Fleming H. Revell Co., n.d.); reprinted as *Lectures on Calvinism* (Grand Rapids: Wm. B. Eerdmans Publishing Co., 1931).

Lake, K., ed. and trans., *The Apostolic Fathers*, vol. II, Loeb Classical Library (Harvard University Press, 1913). Contains the letter concerning the death of Polycarp.

Lilla, M., *The Stillborn God: Religion, Politics, and the Modern West* (New York: Vintage Books, 2008).

Locke, J., *John Locke: Political Writings*, ed. D. Wooton (Indianapolis: Hackett Publishing Co., 1993).

Muffs, Y., *The Personhood of God: Biblical Theology, Human Faith and the Divine Image* (Woodstock, VT: Jewish Lights Publishing Co., 2005).

Murray, J. C., *We Hold These Truths: Catholic Reflections on the American Proposition* (1960; reprinted Lanham, MD: Rowman & Littlefield, 2005).

Novak, M., *Democracy and Mediating Structures: A Theological Inquiry* (Washington, DC: American Enterprise Institute, 1980).

O'Donovan O., and J. L. O'Donovan, eds. and trans., *From Irenaeus to Grotius: A Sourcebook in Christian Political Thought 100–1625* (Grand Rapids: Wm. B. Eerdmans Publishing Co., 1999).

Przywara, E., SJ, ed. and trans., *An Augustine Synthesis* (New York: Sheed & Ward, 1936).

Simmons, A. J., *Moral Principles and Political Obligations* (Princeton University Press, 1979).

Simon, Y., *A General Theory of Authority* (University of Notre Dame Press, 1980).

Smith, S. D., *The Disenchantment of Secular Discourse* (Cambridge, MA: Harvard University Press, 2010).

Stout, J., *Democracy and Tradition* (Princeton University Press, 2004).

Tierney, B., *The Crisis of Church and State: 1050–1300: With Selected Documents* (Englewood Cliffs, NJ: Prentice-Hall, 1964; reprinted University of Toronto Press, 1988).

Van Drunen, D., *Natural Law and the Two Kingdoms: A Study in the Development of Reformed Social Thought* (Grand Rapids: Wm. B. Eerdmans Publishing Co., 2010).

Walzer, M., *Spheres of Justice: A Defense of Pluralism and Equality* (New York: Basic Books, 1983).

Witte, J., *The Reformation of Rights: Law, Religion, and Human Rights in Early Modern Calvinism* (Cambridge University Press, 2007).

Wolterstorff, N., *Divine Discourse* (Cambridge University Press, 1995).

"A Discussion of Oliver O'Donovan's *Desire of the Nations*," *Scottish Journal of Theology*, 54:1 (2001), 87–109.

Justice: Rights and Wrongs (Princeton University Press, 2008).

Justice in Love (Grand Rapids: Wm. B. Eerdmans Publishing Co., 2011).

Understanding Liberal Democracy, ed. T. Cuneo (Oxford University Press, forthcoming).

"'For the Authorities are God's Servants': Is a Theistic Account of Political Authority Still Viable or Have Humanist Accounts Won the Day?" in K. Grasso and C. Castillo, eds., *Theology and Public Philosophy* (Lanham, MD: Rowman & Littlefield, forthcoming).

Yoder, J. H., *The Politics of Jesus: Vicit agnus noster* (Grand Rapids: Wm. B. Eerdmans Publishing Co., 1972; 2nd edn., 1994).

Index of biblical references

General index

CPSIA information can be obtained at www.ICGtesting.com
Printed in the USA
LVOW05s1137210214

374575LV00006B/207/P